Napoleon's Polish Gamble

Campaign Chronicles

Napoleon's Polish Gamble
Eylau and Friedland 1807

Christopher Summerville

Campaign Chronicle
Series Editor

Christopher Summerville

Pen & Sword
MILITARY

To Misia, with love

First published in Great Britain in 2005 by
Pen & Sword Military
an imprint of
Pen & Sword Books Ltd
47 Church Street
Barnsley
South Yorkshire
S70 2AS

Copyright © Christopher Summerville 2005

ISBN 1-84415-260-X

Typeset in Garamond 11/13.5 pt by
Mac Style, Nafferton, E. Yorkshire

Printed and bound in England by CPI UK

For a complete list of Pen & Sword titles, please contact
Pen & Sword Books Limited
47 Church Street, Barnsley, South Yorkshire, S70 2AS, England
E-mail: enquiries@pen-and-sword.co.uk
Website: www.pen-and-sword.co.uk

Contents

List of Illustrations
and Maps

List of Illustrations and Maps

Maps

Author's Note

— ◦—•(•)•—◦ —

I should like to state at the outset that figures given for troop strengths and casualties are approximations only. They are based on statistics quoted in Western sources – including David Chandler, George F. Nafziger, F. Loraine Petre, Digby Smith and Sir Robert Wilson – that I have usually adjusted to the nearest round figure. Where sizeable variations occur, a rough mean average is given. It should be noted that 'casualties' refer to men killed, wounded, sick, and 'missing'. Needless to say, a number of those listed as wounded or sick recovered to fight another day, just as many of the 'missing' eventually turned up to rejoin their units. In other words, the effective strength of the opposing armies was in a constant state of flux, making precise head- and body-counts almost impossible.

The theatre of operations encompassed what was then West, South, and East Prussia – possessions of the Hohenzollern monarchs of Brandenburg–Prussia, whose capital was Berlin. With the exception of East Prussia, this land had been plundered from the ancient kingdom of Poland during the seventeenth and eighteenth centuries: consequently a mix Polish and German names was imposed on the landscape, as reflected in contemporary sources. For the reader's convenience, therefore, a list of German place names with present-day Polish (and in some cases Russian or Lithuanian) equivalents is provided as an appendix. Meanwhile, it should be noted that in the main, 'Preussisch-Eylau' (present-day Bagrationovsk) has been shortened to 'Eylau'.

Finally, I would like to thank those who have helped and supported me during the preparation of this book: Tony Broughton, Robert Burnham, Greg Gorsuch, Rupert Harding, Ewa Haren, Dr Martin Howard, Alexander Mikaberidze, Jonathan North, Stephen Millar and Ken Trotman Ltd.

C.J. Summerville
York 2005

Background

⋯⋅◉⋅⋯

Mind, body, spirit. These are the three elements to our story. The 'mind' constitutes the political and military objectives of the rivals, and particularly those of Napoleon Bonaparte, whose strategical vision drives the campaign. The 'body' is the theatre of operations itself, formed by the carcass of the once-great kingdom of Poland, dismembered by powerful neighbours and awaiting resurrection. The 'spirit' is the animating force behind the actions of the soldiers: Frenchmen fighting for Napoleon's ambition; Russians fighting for the tsar's honour; Poles fighting for freedom; Prussians fighting for their lives. And all attempting to survive in the harshest conditions imaginable.

The Polish Campaign of 1806–07 is widely regarded as one of the bitterest conflicts of the nineteenth century. For some, it was a war of conquest; for others a war of liberation; for most a war of extermination. But for Napoleon, it was a war of wits: for his ultimate aim in Poland was not the liberation of an oppressed people, but the fettering of a free mind to his own will – the mind in question being that of Alexander, tsar of Russia.

Climate of Conflict

On 2 December 1804 Napoleon Bonaparte crowned himself emperor of the French. This theatrical event marked the end of eleven years of war fought in the name of 'Revolution', while raising the curtain on a further eleven, fought in the name of 'Empire'.

To the dynastic heads of Europe, Bonaparte was an 'upstart', an 'adventurer', and perhaps worst of all – as the Duke of Wellington famously observed – 'no gentleman'. A fact illustrated by the abduction, 'trial' and execution of the hapless Bourbon prince, Louis Antoine de Bourbon-Condé, duc d'Enghien, on 15 March 1804. An act of terror designed to overawe his Royalist adversaries – who continued to hatch murderous plots against him – Napoleon's liquidation of d'Enghien (a suspected plotter, but in the event totally innocent) had the desired effect. But the d'Enghien affair sent shockwaves through the drawing rooms of Europe, unleashing a howl of outrage from blue bloods already convinced Bonaparte was the bastard child of the Revolution.

Napoleon's Polish Gamble

Frederick William III (1770–1840). Son of Frederick William II and great-nephew of Frederick the Great. A pacifist who took Prussia to war with France against his will.

had been acquired by the Duchy of Brandenburg, whose powerful Hohenzollern dynasty – electors of the Holy Roman Empire – reigned at Berlin. In 1701, the elector of Brandenburg was crowned Frederick I, 'king-in-Prussia', and by the time of his death, twelve years later, Brandenburg–Prussia was considered the most powerful state in Europe. The aggrandizement of Prussia continued under Frederick's grandson, Frederick II, the 'Great' (ruling from 1740–86), who enlarged his domain with territories plundered from the ancient kingdom of Poland. This trend continued unabated until 1795, when Poland literally disappeared off the map: gobbled up by her three powerful neighbours, Prussia, Russia, and Austria. For her part, Prussia took Posen and Danzig, adding them to Pomerania to form 'West Prussia'; plus the province of Mazovia (including the capital of Warsaw), which was added to Silesia (acquired in the 1740s) to form 'South Prussia'. Meanwhile, the original Baltic duchy of Prussia was renamed 'East Prussia'. Thus, when Frederick II's great-nephew, Frederick William III, ascended the throne in 1797, Berlin was the capital of an engorged Prussian state. Master of the old lands of Brandenburg–Prussia, augmented by successive Polish acquisitions, Frederick William's realm stretched from the Elbe to the Niemen.

But Frederick William III was nothing like his formidable great-uncle. Even-tempered, fair-minded and peace-loving, Frederick William began his reign by reforming Prussia's repressive legal system and improving the country's finances. While the Revolutionary Wars blazed away to the west, Frederick William kept his head down, determined to be left in peace. Even during the War of the Third Coalition – fought in Prussia's backyard – Frederick William refused to be dragged into the conflagration, remaining firmly seated on the fence. But Napoleon's victory at Austerlitz changed everything.

Napoleon was now master of Europe: a latter-day Charlemagne, able to create and destroy empires at will. Following Austria's humiliating reverses in 1805, Napoleon dismantled Vienna's Holy Roman Empire and replaced it with his own Confederation of the Rhine. With this clutch of German states – including Bavaria, Württemberg, Hesse-Darmstadt and Baden – bolted firmly to France, Napoleon was now, effectively, in Frederick William's neighbourhood: soon he would be knocking at the front door.

Napoleon's campaign to drag Frederick William off the fence began with the demand for a formal alliance against Britain. The Prussian king reluctantly agreed, suddenly finding himself at war with a nation that had done him no harm. Having thus bound Prussia to France, Napoleon then demanded – and obtained – the Prussian territories of Cleves, Ansbach and Neufchâtel. By way

Pomerania and Silesia

Pomerania was an ancient Slavonic territory, stretching along the Baltic coast. In 1648 it was divided between Sweden and Brandenburg: the former power taking land west of the River Oder, the latter that to the east. Nevertheless, the ethnic Poles enjoyed a degree of independence, as in previous times. But with the rise of Prussia in the eighteenth century, Sweden's slice was reduced to a small sliver of coastline around the port of Stralsund. During the Partitions of Poland (1772–95) Prussia added Posen and the port of Danzig to Pomerania to create 'West Prussia'.

Silesia was also an ancient Slavonic stronghold, belonging first to Poland and then to Bohemia. In the seventeenth century it fell under Austrian cultural and political influence, only to be conquered by Prussia in the 1740s. When Prussia bagged the Polish province of Mazovia (including the capital of Warsaw) during the Polish partitions, it was added to Silesia to create 'South Prussia'.

of compensation, Prussia was offered the neighbouring state of Hanover, a hereditary possession of the Georgian kings of England. Needless to say, the Prussians were happy to oblige, and Frederick William continued dancing to Napoleon's tune. But without warning, Napoleon pulled the rug from under Frederick William's feet: for without consulting his newfound Prussian friend, Napoleon reneged on the Hanover deal, snatching it back and offering it to Britain's George III – the rightful owner – in return for renewed peace talks. As it happened, the British were unimpressed, being interested neither in Hanover nor peace on Napoleon's terms. The effect on Prussian prestige, however, may be imagined. A further slap in the face for Frederick William occurred on 12 July 1806, when sixteen German princes signed up to Napoleon's Confederation of the Rhine, pledging some 63,000 troops for service with the French Grand Army. Blood boiled in Berlin: it seemed Napoleon was determined to become emperor of Europe, with Prussia not so much an associate as a subordinate. Many must have wondered what Frederick William's great-uncle would have done.

But according to historian, Sebastian Haffner, Frederick William was a genuine pacifist: 'He wanted to remain a simple king of Prussia, and above all he wanted to be left in peace. If there was to be war he did not wish to be responsible.' But the repeated dollops of humble pie doled out by Napoleon had thrown Prussia into turmoil. Consequently, Frederick William's court divided into two opposing camps: the 'Peace Party' and the 'War Party'. Interestingly, the former group was headed by the king himself, and the latter by his beautiful – and spirited – wife, Louise, who reputedly denied her husband conjugal rights until he chose 'the path of honour'. Haffner, however, claims the deciding factor in Frederick William's decision to go to war was his realization that: 'once allied to Napoleon, he would not in the long run be able to escape war against his friend, the tsar.' Meanwhile, a contemporary observer, Karl Wilhelm Ferdinand von Funck (adjutant-general to the king of Saxony), recorded that: 'Frederick William III only decided on war for fear of popular discontent, or rather of the revolutionary faction in Prussia … but always cherished the secret hope that Napoleon would shirk a struggle with the erstwhile military prestige of Prussia and, as soon as he saw things looking serious, negotiate for the repurchase of Prussian friendship.' Whatever the truth of the matter, the time had come for Frederick William – isolated, humiliated, henpecked, and bound by treaty to an ally he could not trust – to jump off the fence.

The Storm Breaks

On 8 August 1806 Frederick William of Prussia mobilized his troops in what historian, E.F. Henderson, describes as: 'a half-hearted way'. The Prussian generals were ordered to muster their men discreetly, taking care not to alarm the

Luise, Queen of Prussia (1776–1810) captured by the artist Grassi in 1802. The beautiful and patriotic wife of Frederick William, who goaded her husband into a disastrous war.

French or provoke them into an attack. For according to Henderson, Frederick William was still hoping for peace, declaring: 'To be sure I do not yet believe that there is any intention on the part of the French to undertake hostilities against us.'

But by mid-September 1806, both Napoleon and Frederick William knew war was inevitable. As a prelude to the conflict, Prussia occupied neighbouring

Napoleon's Polish Gamble

Saxony and absorbed its army: thus denying Napoleon's Confederation of the Rhine 20,000 excellent troops. On 6 October, Prussia strengthened her position by signing a treaty with Russia, Britain, Sweden, and Portugal, thus establishing the British-financed Fourth Coalition. Meanwhile, accusations, insults, demands and ultimata were freely traded between Berlin and Paris, as both sides prepared for bloodshed.

On 8 October Napoleon was ready to strike and the talking stopped. Having concentrated his Grand Army in north-east Bavaria, Bonaparte launched a lightning strike into Prussia, taking Frederick William and his commanders completely by surprise. Six days later it was all over: the Prussian Army – pride of Frederick William's illustrious great-uncle and the scourge of eighteenth century Europe – was annihilated at the Battles of Jena and Auerstädt, both fought on 14 October. According to Bonaparte, the Prussians had 'vanished like an autumn mist before the rising of the sun'. A merciless pursuit of the broken Prussian forces followed, and with stupefying rapidity Frederick William's kingdom collapsed, as town after town fell to the invaders. Within a week Berlin was in Napoleon's hands, and Prussia, as the emperor put it, 'ceased to exist'.

According to Napoleon's theory of warfare, once a nation's field army had been defeated and its capital occupied, capitulation was bound to follow. But it was in his blackest hour that Frederick William found courage, and instead of suing for peace, fled with his family to the old Prussian stronghold of Königsberg, on the Baltic, determined to continue the fight with the aid of the tsar. And so, on 26 October, Napoleon found himself in residence at Berlin's Charlottenburg Palace, but with a war still on his hands. Although the emperor was master of Prussian territory between the Elbe and the Oder, beyond the banks of the latter lay Frederick William's Polish possessions. And beyond Poland, of course, lay Russia. Thus, as historian, John G. Gallagher, observes: 'The victory over the Prussian Army did not bring an end to the war. Frederick William refused to make peace with the French … Thus the campaign entered a second phase, often referred to as the "Polish Campaign", or as Napoleon preferred … the "Polish War of Liberation"'.

Napoleon's Polish Gamble

And so the war continued as Tsar Alexander – who had originally perceived his role in the Fourth Coalition as something of a support act to Prussia – prepared to take centre stage. By 4 November 1806 a Russian Army some 68,000-strong was marching west from Grodno, with the aim of joining the rump of the Prussian field army under General Lestocq. A second Russian force of over 37,000 would soon follow. Furthermore, the fortresses of West, South, and East Prussia were still in Frederick William's hands, while the British Royal Navy prowled the Baltic.

Background

Alexander I (1777–1825). An autocrat with liberal and mystical tendencies, always on the look-out for a new guru, Alexander began the campaign as Napoleon's enemy and finished it under his spell. Nevertheless, Napoleon later said of him, 'He has wit and grace; he is educated, and he has a seductive personality. But he should not be trusted: he lacks frankness, he is a true Byzantine Greek.'

Meanwhile, Napoleon's troops – spearheaded by Marshal Davout's III Corps – had already crossed the Oder, their liberation of Posen provoking a wild outburst of Polish nationalism. The 1st Chasseurs à Cheval, under Colonel (later General) Exelmans, had been the first French regiment to enter town, trotting into the market square as dusk fell, there to be mobbed by an emotional crowd of patriots. But it was the appearance, two days later, of General Dabrowski – leader of Napoleon's Polish Legion – that truly ignited Polish passions, as, assuming the role of recruiting sergeant at Posen, he threw down a challenge: 'I want to see whether the Poles deserve to be a nation!' Within days, Dabrowski was forming four new regiments of infantry, plus two of cavalry: wealthy citizens providing the cash to clothe and equip the ardent volunteers.

Napoleon's Polish Gamble

Thus, despite the French victories of 14 October, Napoleon was forced to accept the war was only just beginning. Although he had huffed and puffed, he had only blown half of Frederick William's house down: for Prussia's Polish lands provided the defeated monarch with a second theatre of operations – one that his Russian allies could enter from the east at will. And that was the crucial point: for if Napoleon allowed Alexander's army freedom of manoeuvre, its advance on the Vistula might well unleash an avalanche of disasters. As Napoleon himself put it: 'If I let the Russians advance I should lose the support and the resources of Poland; they might decide Austria, which only hesitated because they were so far off; they would carry with them the whole Prussian nation, which would feel the necessity of doing everything it could to retrieve its disasters.' In other words, Napoleon was obliged to grab the territory between the Oder and the Vistula in order to deny its resources to the advancing Russians, prevent a Prussian recovery, and keep Austria in check. Consequently, as Bonaparte's biographer, Bourrienne, observes: 'he [Napoleon] resolved to commence a winter campaign in a climate more rigorous than any in which he had hitherto fought … Skilful above every other general in the choice of his fields of battle, he was not willing to await tranquilly until the Russian Army, which was advancing towards Germany, should come to measure its strength with him in the plains of conquered

Dabrowski's Mazurka

Following the failure of the Kosciuszko Insurrection of 1794 – a direct response to the dismemberment of their country at the hands of Prussia, Russia and Austria – many Poles scattered throughout Europe. Many emigrated to Revolutionary France, a kind of 'spiritual home' whose enemies were also Poland's persecutors.

Among these was Jan Henryk Dabrowski (pronounced 'Dombrowski', which is how it is sometimes spelt in English sources). Born near Krakow, but raised and educated in Saxony, Dabrowski became a general in the French Army. He raised a Polish Legion in 1795 for service in Italy, comprised of fellow émigrés and deserters from the Austrian Army. A marching song was composed by Jozef Wybicki for the occasion of Dabrowski's departure for the front, beginning with the words: 'Poland is not yet lost while we live, We will fight with swords for all that our enemies have taken from us.' The song – originally entitled 'Song of the Polish Legions in Italy' eventually became known as 'Dabrowski's Mazurka', and was adopted by patriots in Poland as an anthem. The song was banned by the Russian authorities during the nineteenth century, but resurfaced to become Poland's National Anthem in 1926.

Background

Prussia; he resolved to march to meet it, and to reach it before it should have crossed the Vistula.'

But with half the Grand Army still mopping up Prussian resistance around Lübeck and Magdeburg, Napoleon was obliged to push Marshals Murat, Davout, Lannes and Augereau towards the Vistula unsupported, with orders to occupy the east bank and establish bridgeheads. Unsure of the Russians' exact location, Napoleon's first thought was simply to buy time for the rest of his army to catch up.

Yet the emperor was not entirely displeased with the turn of events. From a grand strategical viewpoint, a golden opportunity had presented itself: for if he could defeat Alexander without undermining his authority – that is to say, without liberating his Polish subjects – then the tsar might be wooed away from friendship with Britain and towards an alliance with France. The idea instantly provided Napoleon with a clear strategical vision, which would underpin his policy in the months to come. First, decisive action regarding the issue of Polish liberation must be avoided, for fear of unduly antagonizing Russia and Austria: the Poles might be offered encouragement in their struggle for liberty but not promises. Second, the Russian Army must be decisively beaten in Poland – annihilated, in fact – thus bringing Alexander to the bargaining table, where he could be manoeuvred into position alongside France via a magnanimous peace. But Napoleon kept these cards close to his chest, and as Norman Davies observes, the Polish campaign would be fought 'without any indication of its political aims.'

But golden opportunities and strategical visions apart, Napoleon's march into Poland – though arguably forced – constituted a daring gamble: for if he failed to crush the Russian Army in a battle of decision, or indeed, overawe Alexander, then he would be stranded 1,000 miles (1,609km) from Paris, in the near-arctic winter of the poorest country in Europe, with a recalcitrant Russia in his face and a hostile Europe at his back. And if he failed to contain the flames of Polish patriotism – already fanned by the presence of his soldiers east of the Oder – they might consume him, and therefore France, in a costly pan-European war.

Meantime, events gathered momentum. On 9 November, Napoleon received word of the final surrender of Prussian forces west of the Oder, with Blücher's capitulation at the free city and Hanseatic port of Lübeck: soon more French troops would be available for the drive into Poland. And with Murat and Davout advancing on Warsaw – leaving the unsubdued fortresses of Silesia in their rear – this was good news indeed. Next day, Napoleon tried his luck at extracting all he desired from Prussia without resorting to further bloodshed. In return for peace, the emperor's impossibly harsh terms included: the surrender of all Prussian territory west of the Elbe, payment of a vast war indemnity, and an alliance against Russia. Needless to say, Frederick William remained defiant: for although General Koehler, the Prussian governor of Warsaw, had recently fled the city at the head of his troops – jeered and stoned by schoolboys – soldiers of the Russian First Army, under General Bennigsen, were about to enter Praga, Warsaw's eastern suburb. The following week, on 21 November, Napoleon opened the eco-war with Britain by announcing: 'The British Isles are declared to be in a state of blockade.' With this phrase, the emperor launched the so-called 'Continental System', which aimed to destroy British industry by closing European markets. It was a fatal step. But having issued his 'Berlin Decrees', Napoleon quit the Prussian capital and blithely marched east, leading his Imperial Guard across the Oder. As Philippe de Ségur, the emperor's aide-de-camp noted: 'The war with Prussia was at an end. The war of Poland against the Russians was beginning …'

Theatre of Operations

In the main, the action of the coming campaign would take place east of the Vistula, in the northern half of what is now the Republic of Poland and the Russian enclave of Kaliningrad. Viewed on the map, the theatre of operations could be described as an enclosure some 200 miles (321.8km) square. The western edge of this war zone was formed by the Vistula, the northern edge by the shores of the Baltic, the eastern edge by the River Niemen, and the southern edge by the Rivers Bug and Vistula. In 1806, the 40,000 square miles (64,372 square km) contained within the zone constituted a flat, boggy plain, intersected by rivers, littered with lakes, and carpeted with thick forests. The principal rivers of the campaign were the Vistula, Passarge, Wkra, Narew, Alle and Niemen. These waterways – when not frozen over – formed barriers to the passage of large armies, and were therefore regarded by both sides as natural bulwarks and lines of defence. As for the lakes, they largely disappeared in winter, their surfaces petrified by frost and hidden by snow to such an extent that unwitting soldiers frequently marched – and even bivouacked – upon them. The forests – home to wolves, bears, lynx and wild boar – were mainly spruce and pine, the largest being the immense Johannisberg Forest, north-east of Warsaw, which covered at least 500 square miles (804.6 square km). The climate was – and is – Continental, with harsh winters and hot summers. Winter comes to Poland from the north-east and this corner of the country is the coldest. On average, there is snow for some 130 days of the year. January is the bleakest month, with temperatures plummeting as low as minus 30 degrees Celsius, and with full daylight existing only between the hours of 7.30 a.m. and 4.00 p.m.

The theatre of operations contained few cities, though the landscape was punctuated with numerous fortresses, most of which, at the beginning of the campaign, were still garrisoned by Prussian troops. Interestingly, the great fortress towns of Danzig, Königsberg, Warsaw, and Thorn were all situated on

Background

Murat Enters Warsaw (contemporary print). The grand duke of Berg entered the old Polish capital on the evening of 28 November 1806 to a rapturous welcome. Viewed as a liberator, Murat was fêted by the Poles, igniting vain hopes of future kingship.

the outer edges of the operational zone: inside was a desert, pock-marked by impoverished villages and towns, linked by unmetalled roads or dirt tracks, where the vast majority of the population subsisted on the scanty fruits of agricultural labour. In fact, as far as the French were concerned, the area appears to have been something of a *terra incognita*, for according to historian, F.D. Logan:

> 'The topography of Poland was little known. A survey detachment directly under imperial headquarters was accordingly organized to which was entrusted the task of mapping the country as the army advanced. The instructions issued to these "surveyors" are not without interest. They were to move with the advanced guard of each corps and to send their work daily to imperial headquarters. Attention was especially called to the necessity for recording the name of each village – this, one would think, was a somewhat superfluous instruction – with its population and nature of soil. Each sketch was to be signed so that, if more precise information was subsequently required by Napoleon, the officer concerned could be readily summoned. The emperor complained later that it was often difficult

Napoleon's Polish Gamble

General Bennigsen (1745–1826). The German in command of the Russian First Army, and later commander-in-chief of the tsar's troops in Poland. According to historian, Edward Foord, Bennigsen was 'a Hanoverian soldier of fortune … He appears to have been a selfish and jealous but able man.'

soldiers belonged to the former group, which traditionally deployed in dense linear formations – hence the term 'line'. Meanwhile, the less numerous light infantry acted as sentries, scouts, skirmishers and sharpshooters. In general, the principal tactical unit was the battalion, which might consist of anything between 500 and 1,500 men. The soldier's 'parent' or administrative unit, however, was the regiment, which usually contained several battalions. Quality varied enormously, depending on national resources and priorities. In many cases, soldiers marched to war with hardly any training at all. Virtually all infantrymen were armed with the muzzle-loading, smooth-bore musket plus bayonet (the manufacture and use of rifles being in its infancy). Due to the gross inaccuracy of flintlock muskets – roughly speaking, a soldier stood a 50 per cent chance of hitting his target at a range of 100 yards (91.4m) – significant damage could only be inflicted upon the enemy by massing troops together in order to deliver mighty death-dealing

Background

Lieutenant General Buxhöwden (1750–1811). Ex-governor of the tsar's Polish territories, Buxhöwden was the courageous commander of the Russian Second Army. Sadly, his relationship with colleague and fellow-German, Bennigsen, was dogged by rivalry, suspicion and jealousy.

volleys. That said, the mere threat of the bayonet by a mass formation could be as effective as its firepower: for the sight of several thousand soldiers advancing with the cold steel had a devastating psychological effect on demoralized men.

Cavalry was also divided into two basic types: 'heavy' and 'light'. This division echoed – at least in theory – the roles of 'line' and 'light' infantry described above. The 'heavy' cavalry regiments – big men riding big horses – being essentially a battlefield weapon; while 'light' horsemen – such as the flamboyant hussars common to most European armies – guarded the front, rear and flanks of an army, performing reconnaissance, outpost and escort duties. This is an oversimplification, however, for in reality distinctions were blurred – or perhaps more correctly, ignored – and most cavalrymen were trained to execute a variety of tasks. Mounted regiments were frequently lumped together into brigades or divisions, but the basic battlefield unit was the squadron, consisting of several hundred troopers. Although capable of fighting as skirmishers, in a major battle cavalry units were usually deployed in line: the idea being to outflank enemy formations, while bringing to bear as many sabres as possible in the initial contact. The light cavalry favoured curved sabres for slashing, while the 'heavies' used a straight blade for thrusting. Cavalrymen might also be armed with a brace of pistols or a short-barrelled carbine. Some mounted troops, like the Polish light cavalry regiments and the celebrated Russian Cossacks, specialized in the use of the lance. Needless to say, the key factor in developing a strong cavalry arm was a good supply of horses: without them, cavalry troopers were simply infantrymen in fancy uniforms. And yet the sheer wastage of horseflesh during the period was staggering, hundreds of thousands of beasts being slaughtered – one way or another – each year. Thus the availability and quality of remounts directly affected the availability and quality of a nation's cavalry.

Artillery was divided into 'foot batteries' and 'horse troops', the latter having lighter guns and mounted crews for greater mobility. Cannon were classified according to the weight of the shot they fired: thus a gun firing a 12lb shot was designated a '12-pounder'. Most battlefield artillery consisted of 4-, 6-, 8-, 9- or 12-pounders, with horse artillery opting for the lighter weights. On average, an eight-man crew operating a 12-pounder could loose off one round per minute: the effective range of the gun being about 1,000 yards (914m). Guns were grouped into batteries of between six and twelve pieces (although the Russians sometimes deployed fourteen-gun batteries), each battery requiring perhaps thirty vehicles, 130 horses and over 100 men to transport, deploy and service it. Batteries were either spread along an army's entire front or concentrated into 'grand batteries'. Either way, once on the battlefield, guns were hauled into place and aimed by sight: this process being repeated after the recoil of each shot. By far the most common projectile was a simple iron ball, known as roundshot. Thundering into densely-packed troop formations, roundshot could wreak havoc, a single ball being capable of killing or maiming up to thirty men. An alternative to roundshot was the dreaded case-shot or 'canister': a tin case packed with bullets (the French reputedly added iron nails), which when fired at close-range, showered attacking troops with a hail of metal.

Sadly, medical care for wounded soldiers was not a priority in Napoleonic armies. A surgeon was usually attached to each battalion, aided by an assistant, but pay was low and as a consequence, so were professional standards. Needless to say, most battlefield casualties were produced by artillery fire, followed by musket fire: the most common form of injury being limb wounds. Every soldier knew that if left untreated, such wounds could become fatal, as the transfer of energy from the projectile to the body resulted in dead tissue, in which bacteria could thrive, leading to septicemia, tetanus and gangrene. The removal of dead tissue by surgery was not possible during Napoleonic times, as anaesthetics were unknown. Thus, amputation of the affected limb was seen by all as the best option. Soldiers were expected to endure the ordeal without complaint, amputations normally being performed by a surgeon armed with a knife – sharp or otherwise. Live maggots were sewn into the wound, where they would quickly consume the remaining dead tissue. Survival after amputation depended upon how quickly the operation was performed, delays proving fatal. That said, around 33 per cent of all amputees died anyway, either on the surgeon's table or soon after leaving hospital.

The Prussian Army

During the reign of Frederick the Great (1740–86) the Prussian Army was nurtured, cultivated and nourished by the inspirational leadership of the warrior-king. By the time of his death, Frederick's army was the envy of Europe, and his concepts regarding army structure, organization, tactics and drill much-copied. But in the 1790s the citizen armies of the French Revolution violated the military model of the Enlightenment era, distorting war from a game of chess into a *jeu sans frontières*: a game without rules. Napoleon Bonaparte – a keen student of Frederick – harnessed the spirit and aggression of the Revolutionary armies, while emphasizing speed and flexibility. Thus, by 1806 war had been – to use Napoleon's word – 'revolutionized'.

The Prussian Army, however, remained rooted in the past: a fossil preserved in Baltic amber. Following the demise of Frederick, subsequent Prussian kings had seen no need to improve on the methods of 'Old Fritz', remaining happy to trade on past glories. Thus, by the time Napoleon blazed onto the scene, Prussia's army was an ossified relic. This statement is amply illustrated by the fact that in 1806, half of the army's generals, and more than a quarter of its regimental and battalion officers, were over sixty years old. No one doubted the fighting qualities of Prussian soldiers: but in 1806 they were poorly led by an elderly, aristocratic officer corps, whose methods were twenty years out of date.

On the eve of war, Prussia had a standing army of some 200,000 men. But within a few short weeks this impressive resource had all-but vanished: 40,000 men were lost at the Battles of Saalfeld, Jena and Auerstädt, and 90,000 (mainly taken prisoner) in the collapse that followed hard on the heels of these disasters, as fortresses fell to the French, almost without a fight. This left some 70,000 soldiers available to Frederick William in Poland. But the bulk of these were stranded in the fortress-towns of Silesia, Pomerania, and East Prussia, leaving General Lestocq's single corps of less than 20,000 men in the field.

The Russian Army

At the turn of the nineteenth century Russia's population was pushing the 50 million mark, so manpower for the army wasn't a problem. Over half of the adult male population were serfs – agricultural labourers literally owned by their aristocratic masters – and as the tsar levied one in twenty for military service, the Russian Army totalled some 500,000 men. But like the Prussian Army, upon

Russian Fusilier 1807 (contemporary print by Edward Orme). According to the tsar's English liaison officer, Sir Robert Wilson, the average Russian infantryman was: 'ferocious but disciplined; obstinately brave, and susceptible of enthusiastic excitements ...'

Background

which it was largely modelled, the Russian Army of 1806 was outdated. Although Alexander had begun a process of modernization upon his accession in 1801, the influence of his father, Paul I, was still in evidence. Tsar Paul had been obsessed with recreating the army of Frederick the Great: consequently, Russian soldiers were endlessly drilled on the parade ground – steel plates strapped round their knees in order to keep their legs straight – while combat performance was neglected. Equipment and weapons were neglected too, the Russian musket being almost twice as heavy as its French counterpart, which weighed in at around 10lbs (4.5kg). It was also inefficient, and if contemporary reports are to be believed, was prone to misfiring. No wonder, then, Russian troops were encouraged to rely on their bayonets.

Fortunately, the raw material of the Russian Army was tough and resilient. In fact, the tsar's serfs – stout, stoical, steadfast – were perfect fodder for the army, and recruits were conscripted for a term of twenty-five years with no leave permitted. According to Sir Robert Wilson, a British liaison officer attached to Alexander's staff, the Russian infantry was composed of:

'athletic men between the ages of eighteen and forty, endowed with great bodily strength, but generally short of stature, with martial countenance and complexion; inured to the extremes of weather and hardship; to the worst and scantiest of food; to marches for days and nights, of four hours repose and six hours

Russian Lifeguard 1807 (contemporary print by Edward Orme). Ceremonial troops that also functioned as armoured heavy cavalry.

21

progress; accustomed to laborious toils, and the carriage of heavy burthens; ferocious but disciplined; obstinately brave, and susceptible of enthusiastic excitements; devoted to their sovereign, their chief, and their country.'

Less enthusiastic beholders, however, highlighted the barbaric treatment of soldiers at the hands of their officers and NCOs, while the French regarded the average Russian as little better than a beast of burden. But perhaps the fairest assessment of Alexander's army is that made by historian, Edward Foord, writing in 1914:

'The characteristics of the Russian soldier have never varied. He was and is endowed with remarkable endurance and courage, but is comparatively unintelligent … illiteracy was practically universal … Life in the ranks was hard, and only the fact that it was probably no harder than the existence of the average peasant could have rendered it endurable. The men were well clothed … but they were in general ill-fed, ill-lodged, ill-cared for, and practically unpaid. The methods of maintaining discipline were brutal …. It is all to their honour that they made … such good soldiers … There is a tendency to regard the Russian soldiers as generally large men, but there is abundant evidence that this was not the case … The guards were picked men. The cavalry, artillery, light infantry and grenadiers absorbed the best remaining recruits; the ordinary line regiments, with very inadequate means, had to assimilate and train the poorest of the available material.'

Alexander's infantry comprised grenadiers, musketeers and *Jägers*. The latter constituted the army's light infantry, recruited in Siberia according to campaign historian, F. Loraine Petre, and 'superior as marksmen to the line regiments'. Each infantry regiment possessed three battalions. Alexander's cavalry – which enjoyed a higher status than the infantry – consisted of well-mounted regular regiments augmented by hordes of 'irregular' Cossacks and Kalmucks (Mongolian tribesmen). The tsar's artillery, meanwhile, was, in the words of Wilson: 'of the most powerful description. No other army moves with so many guns, and with no other army is it in a better state of equipment, or is more gallantly served.' Despite this impressive picture, however, the army was underfunded. Consequently, medical, supply and support services were sorely neglected, Wilson himself lamenting that: 'The commissariat is wretched …'

And if contemporary observers are to be believed, so was the Russian Army's officer corps: for if the ordinary Russian soldiers – the so-called *moujiks* – constituted first-class martial material, their officers – despite their nobility –

were generally regarded as third-class. Even the pro-Russian Wilson paints a less than impressive picture: 'The Russian officer, although frequently making the greatest physical exertions, is, however, inclined to indolent habits when not on actual duty; he loves his sleep after food, and dislikes to walk or ride far. His general mode of conveyance is in a waggon, even when passing from one cantonment to another.' Although undoubtedly brave and gallant, the average Russian officer was not, it seems, on a par with his French counterpart. Apparently addicted to drinking, gambling and sleeping, pundits of the era conjure up an image of a recklessly intoxicated, soporiferous aristocrat. Even at the higher levels of command ineptitude was rife – as was bitter rivalry and petty jealousy. Alexander's solution was to include foreigners (especially Germans) among his top brass: dubbed 'scientific soldiers', they were generally despised by their Russian colleagues.

The Russian forces that marched into Poland to meet Napoleon were initially split into two separate commands: the First Army, under General Bennigsen, and the Second Army, under Lieutenant General Buxhöwden. At first, the command-in-chief was exercized by Marshal Kamenskoi, then briefly passed to Buxhöwden, before finally resting with Bennigsen. According to Petre, Bennigsen's First Army consisted of 49,000 infantry, 11,000 cavalry, 4,000 Cossacks, 2,700 artillerymen, and 900 pioneers: making a total of 68,000 men augmented by 276 guns. Buxhöwden's Second Army consisted of 29,000 infantry, 7,000 cavalry, 1,200 artillerymen: making a total of 37,200 men augmented by 216 guns. Thus, at the outset of the campaign, the grand total of Russian troops in theatre was 105,200 men and 492 guns. Later, Alexander would throw in reserves, including over 12,000 troops from his brother, the Grand Duke Constantine's 1st (Imperial Guard) Division.

As for the generals in charge of the campaign, Marshal Kamenskoi was a 75-year-old veteran who, according to Petre, 'was now too old for war'. Lieutenant General Friedrich Wilhelm Buxhöwden was the 57-year-old ex-governor of Russia's Polish territories. An Estonian German who married an illegitimate daughter of Catherine the Great, Buxhöwden was a courageous – if somewhat lacklustre – commander. If nothing else, however, Buxhöwden campaigned in style, encumbered with an enormous train of servants and hunting dogs. As for General Count Levin A.T. Bennigsen, he was a 62-year-old Hanoverian who had entered Russian service in 1773. Generally acknowledged as a capable cavalry leader, Bennigsen was somewhat out of his depth as an army commander, matters not being helped by his bitter rivalry with Buxhöwden. According to Petre, Bennigsen 'can hardly be described as a great general … For the partial successes which he obtained in this campaign against the French, the valour and obstinacy of his troops, rather than his tactics, account.'

Napoleon's Polish Gamble

The French Army

Following the French victories at Jena and Auerstädt, Napoleon had over 200,000 troops at his immediate disposal with which to prosecute the Polish war. Many were veterans of earlier campaigns; most had just participated in the annihilation of the Prussian field army. But as Petre observes, the French troops: 'were now preparing for a renewed war against fresh enemies; the hardest task that an army can undertake. Even these hardened and enthusiastic warriors contemplated with dread the prospect of a fresh winter campaign in an inhospitable and difficult country, and Napoleon was often remonstrated with, as he rode alongside of his men, for insisting on their advance into Poland.' Indeed, it is fair to say that from the outset, morale among the French conscripts was low: for having entered Berlin in triumph – enough, in the soldiers' eyes, to terminate the war – they were promptly pushed east towards the Vistula and into the teeth of an oncoming Russian Army, dragging winter along with it.

Nevertheless, according to F.D. Logan: 'The French Army at the commencement of the campaign was almost at its zenith. Cavalry, artillery, and infantry were all well trained and equipped.' None more so, perhaps, than the artillery, which had been steadily evolving into a major military asset since the 1770s. Jean-Baptiste Gribeauval had begun the process, and Napoleon – an ex-artillery officer – had completed it. Thus, by 1806 the French artillery arm had been completely modernized, with guns redesigned, lightened, their calibres standardized, and their sights and inclination markers improved. Transportation, meanwhile, had been taken out of the hands of civilian drivers and placed under army control for greater efficiency. As for the French gunners, they were exhaustively trained to maintain rapid fire, and whenever possible, to increase its effectiveness by closing with the enemy. Batteries were distributed throughout the various army corps, but Napoleon kept 25 per cent of available artillery in a central reserve, under his personal direction.

According to the emperor: 'The French soldier possesses bravery of an impatient sort and a sense of honour that makes him capable of the greatest efforts; but he is in need of severe discipline and he must not be left idle for long.' The infantry, therefore – of which Napoleon had some 172,00 at the start of the Polish campaign – was worked excessively hard, some 100 soldiers actually being driven to suicide by Christmas Day 1806. The foot soldiers' load included knapsack, water bottle, cooking pot, blanket or greatcoat, entrenching tool, musket and ammunition: a total weight of over 60lbs (27kg). And yet, the French infantryman was expected to march faster and farther than his European counterparts. According to Elzéar Blaze: 'We marched to the right, to the left, to the front, sometimes to the rear. We always marched. Very often we didn't know why …' An average march – roads permitting – covered 15 miles (24km) a day, though forced marches of double this distance were not uncommon. The rate of

Background

French Line Infantry, circa 1808. The figure on the left is a grenadier: élite troops picked for strength and bravery. The figure on the right is a voltigeur: *light infantrymen deployed as skirmishers.*

French Line Infantry. The backbone of Napoleon's army, he began the campaign with over 150,000 but soon wanted more.

Background

French Light Cavalry (Edouard Detaille). These flamboyant hussars and chasseurs *were expected to reconnoitre in advance of the army's line of march, functioning as its eyes and ears. But bad weather and execrable roads hampered their operations in Poland, rendering the Grand Army blind.*

march was generally the *pas ordinaire*, set by regulations at seventy-six steps per minute. A brief halt was called every five hours, the so-called *haltes des pipes*, as soldiers generally snatched a swift smoke. Around midday a *grande haltes* of one hour was called for food. And yet, following Napoleon's maxim that 'War must feed war,' French soldiers were expected to survive on the resources of the countryside through which they passed. Should supplies be scarce, however, the emperor at least was not unduly worried, for he apparently believed that: 'The French soldier is the only European soldier who can fight on an empty stomach.' A boast that would be put to the test in the Polish winter of 1806–07. On the battlefield, French troops were required to manoeuvre en masse – at the regulation speed of 120 paces per minute – in line, column or a combination of the two: the so-called *ordre mixte*. In the attack, conscripts were required to follow their officers – who always led from the front – hearts pounding to the beat of the *pas de charge*.

As for Napoleon's mounted troops, according to David Johnson, in *Napoleon's Cavalry and its Leaders*: 'No other cavalry force in history was led so brilliantly and handled so badly.' A reference, no doubt, to the limitations of Napoleon's cavalry supremo, Joachim Murat, who in Petre's words: 'was the beau ideal of the leader of a cavalry charge. Yet he was not, in any sense, a great cavalry general.' In other words, Murat knew how to risk the lives of his men and horses, but not how to save them. Nevertheless, Napoleon's cavalry was a formidable weapon, and one the emperor believed capable of winning battles. For though each army corps had a cavalry brigade or division attached, Napoleon maintained a powerful central reserve for use as a tactical resource in moments of crisis. But on a day-to-day basis, as historian, John R. Elting, explains, the French mounted regiments were employed as follows: 'The light cavalry formed a screen behind which the Grande Armée manoeuvred, hunting down the enemy and driving in the enemy cavalry's scouts and patrols. Dragoon divisions might be employed to stiffen this screen … or to cover the army's flanks as it drove deeper into hostile territory. The heavy cavalry was held intact for the day of battle, then launched as massed projectiles to smash and shatter the enemy's line.'

But perhaps the major strength of the Grand Army lay in its organization: for while other armies lumbered around Europe as single, monstrous entities, the French host was sub-divided into several self-contained corps. The system was not new (the army of Ancient Rome operated on a similar principle) and was not even resurrected by Napoleon: for the concept had been tested by French commanders of the 1740s and 1770s. But – as with the artillery reforms of Gribeauval – Bonaparte built his own house on someone else's foundations, honing the concept during his army reforms of 1802–04. The result was the adoption of the army corps as the basic strategic and grand tactical unit of the French Army. In fact, each corps was nothing less than a miniature army, consisting of the usual building-blocks of infantry, cavalry, artillery, and augmented by supporting services – engineers, medical, and so on – as well as a small staff. Each individual corps was commanded by a senior general or marshal, but the aggregate remained under Napoleon's personal direction. Being a self-contained unit, a single corps was capable of holding its own against a superior force for several days, thus buying time for Napoleon to deploy the remainder of his army as circumstances demanded. The system also meant French forces could march in a dispersed fashion, each corps making best use of available roads and resources, before concentrating for battle. Furthermore, the axis of advance or retreat could be changed at a moment's notice: the various corps switching roles as advance guard, right-wing, left-wing, centre and rearguard. The key to maintaining overall army cohesion, was to keep each corps within a single day's march of its neighbour. Thus, for a time – for his system was soon copied – Napoleon enjoyed increased speed, manoeuvrability and flexibility over his enemies. At the outset of the Polish campaign, the Grand Army was made up of the following corps:

I Corps, consisting of 22,000 men and commanded by Marshal Bernadotte
III Corps, consisting of 23,000 men and commanded by Marshal Davout
IV Corps, consisting of 28,000 men and commanded by Marshal Soult
V Corps, consisting of 18,000 men and commanded by Marshal Lannes
VI Corps, consisting of 18,000 men and commanded by Marshal Ney
VII Corps, consisting of 17,000 men and commanded by Marshal Augereau
VIII Corps, consisting of 12,000 men and commanded by Marshal Mortier
IX Corps, consisting of 22,000 men and commanded by Jérôme Bonaparte

In January 1807 Napoleon created X Corps, consisting of 26,000 men. General Victor was earmarked for command of this force, but as he was captured by Prussians that same month, Marshal Lefebvre was moved from the Imperial Guard to take his place (Victor was released on 8 March 1807 – exchanged for Blücher, the future Waterloo hero – but Lefebvre retained command of X Corps). Meanwhile, Marmont's II Corps was stationed in Dalmatia and therefore out of the theatre of operations.

As for 'Les Gros Bonnets' ('The Big Hats') as Napoleon's corps commanders were affectionately known: Augereau – a good tactician – was the uneducated son of a stone mason; Bernadotte – 'Calm, selfish, calculating, and astute' (Petre) – the son of a lawyer; Jérôme – the youngest and perhaps least talented of the Bonaparte brothers – the son of a lawyer; Davout – 'a fine example of the modern scientific soldier, a stern disciplinarian and an admirable administrator' (Foord) – the son of an officer; Lannes – a loyal and courageous ex-grenadier, who 'feared neither the enemy nor the emperor' (Petre) – the son of a peasant; Lefebvre – 'A hard-headed, courageous old soldier' (Petre) – the son of a miller; Mortier – a half-English general 'of average capacity' (Petre) – the son of a farmer; Ney – the insubordinate hothead, who as a corps commander was 'probably unsurpassed' (Foord) – the son of a barrel-maker; Soult – perhaps Napoleon's most capable lieutenant – the son of a lawyer. With the exception of the youthful Jérôme, they were all veterans of the Revolutionary Wars, learning their trade at the cannon's mouth. As acolytes of the emperor, they had received fancy titles and great wealth: in return, Napoleon demanded loyalty, obedience, and the tireless pursuit of victory.

Prussian Infantry Officer 1806 (painting by J.A. Langendyke). The uniform is similar to that worn under Frederick the Great, reflecting the outmoded nature of the army and its elderly officer corps.

Background

Other top brass included Marshal Berthier (son of an engineer, now Prince of Neufchâtel), the uncharismatic but supremely capable chief of staff; and Marshal Murat (son of an innkeeper, now grand duke of Berg), the not-so-capable but supremely charismatic leader of the Cavalry Reserve. And lording it over the lot, like a latter-day Caesar, was the emperor himself: combining the roles of commander-in-chief and head of state in one person.

Space does not permit a detailed examination of Napoleon's remarkable career or personality: suffice it to say that by 1806 his reputation as a great captain was already established. As the conqueror of Italy and Egypt in the 1790s, and the victor of Austerlitz in 1805, Bonaparte had proved himself a

Napoleon's Marshals

On 19 May 1804 Napoleon created eighteen marshals of the empire. The post was more of an appointment than a military rank, the senior army grade remaining general of division. But as emperor, Napoleon needed an aristocracy, and the marshals were to be his acolytes. Napoleon lavished wealth, honours and titles upon his marshals: binding their fortunes to ensure loyalty. According to historian, R.P. Dunn-Pattison: 'It was on 19 May 1804 that the *Gazette* appeared with the first creation of marshals. There were fourteen on the active list and four honorary marshals in the Senate. Two bâtons were withheld a reward for future service. The original fourteen were Berthier, Murat, Moncey, Jourdan, Masséna, Augereau, Bernadotte, Soult, Brune, Lannes, Mortier, Ney, Davout and Bessières; while on the retired list were Kellermann, Lefebvre, Pérignon, and Serurier … By the end of the Empire, death and the necessity of rewarding merit added to the list of marshals until in all twenty-six batons were granted by the emperor.'

But with wealth and status came egotism, envy, greed and jealousy. And as often as not, Napoleon's marshals were at each others' throats rather than the enemy's. Napoleon soon wearied of the antics of his élite, claiming: 'Those people think they are indispensable; they don't know that I have a hundred division commanders who can take their place.' And yet, the emperor cynically used the levers of vanity and self-interest to control the marshals, a policy noted by Saxon soldier-diplomat, von Funck: 'There were intrigues of jealousy … among the leaders of his armies, that might go so far that one general would have welcomed the other's defeat, or failed to support him in a crisis; but they all had to cower before the master's eye; and the emperor, reviewing them astutely, contrived – for it was rare for him to punish – to convert private jealousies into rivalry in his service. Thus, Davout and Bernadotte, Masséna and Savary, were at daggers drawn; hardly any marshal had a good word to say for any other; but all of them served the emperor and the honour of his name with equal zeal.'

Russian Cossacks (aquatint by G. Schadow). English observer, Sir Robert Wilson, describes Cossack troopers thus: 'Mounted on a very little, ill-conditioned, but well-bred horse … with a

short whip on his wrist (as he wears no spur) – armed with the lance, a pistol in his girdle, and a sword, he never fears a competitor in single combat …'

military genius. And through a combination of hard work, good fortune, and natural ability, Napoleon had risen from an obscure lieutenant of artillery to the emperor of France within the space of twenty years. But it was not enough. Bonaparte was a student of history, an admirer of Caesar and Alexander, and his ambition was to found an empire to rival those of his heroes. Thus, as Frank Mclynn observes: 'in 1806 there are many pointers to a new, harsher Napoleon, who would brook no opposition and whose attitude to dissent anticipated the dictatorships of the twentieth century.'

As to Napoleon's qualities, he was a man of many parts, and despite his declaration that 'I am not a person, I am thing,' he was, in fact, many 'things' to many people. For some he was a student ('Read and meditate upon the wars of the greatest captains. This is the only means of rightly learning the science of war'), a thinker ('Whatever has not been profoundly meditated in all its details is totally ineffectual'), a visionary ('Imagination rules the world'), a revolutionary ('I have fought like a lion for the Republic'), a national hero ('Everything for the French people'), a master strategist ('I see only one thing, namely, the enemy's main body: I will try to crush it, confident that secondary matters will then settle themselves'), a genius ('God has given me the power and will to overcome all obstacles'), even a superman ('Impossible – a word found only in the dictionary of fools'); for others, he was an adventurer ('I aimed at the empire of the world; who in my place would not have done the same?'), a braggart ('I am not an ordinary man, and the laws of morals and of custom were never made for me'), a cynic ('Men are moved by two levers only: fear and self-interest'), a dictator ('Power is my mistress'), a butcher ('Troops are made to let themselves be killed'), a monster ('War justifies everything') and a grand disturber ('A man like me only ceases to be formidable when he is laid in the tomb'). For the men of the Grand Army, however, he was 'Our Comrade' – a *confrère*, who understood soldiers and communicated in their language: 'A man does not have himself killed for a few halfpence a day … you must speak to the soul in order to electrify the man.'

If Napoleon was essentially a wannabe Caesar, then it should come as no surprise that he augmented his army with foreign auxiliaries and a Praetorian Guard of sorts. This latter formation, the Imperial Guard, was, as Philip Haythornthwaite describes in *Imperial Guardsman 1799–1815*: 'one of the most famous military formations in history, and quite distinct from the guard corps of other European sovereigns of the period. The Imperial Guard could perform ceremonial duties as well as any, but it was primarily an élite combat formation.' In fact, Napoleon's Imperial Guard was an army-within-an-army: a force of all arms, loyal to his person, which the emperor was keen to preserve. Thus, Napoleon pampered his Guard and rarely committed it to battle, keeping it instead as his ultimate reserve. As a consequence, Imperial Guardsmen were both envied and despised by the less fortunate soldiers of the line, who nicknamed them 'The Immortals' because their lives were seldom risked in action. At the start of the Polish campaign the Imperial Guard numbered some 10,000 troops: the infantry initially under the command of Marshal Lefebvre, the cavalry under Marshal Bessières.

As for his auxiliaries, although Napoleon managed to scrape together a handful of troops from satellite states such as Spain, Italy and Holland, most came from the German states of the Confederation of the Rhine: Bavaria, Baden, Hesse and Württemberg, all providing troops – a total of perhaps 20,000 – which Napoleon put under the command of his youngest brother, Jérôme. But as Bourrienne explains, the Confederation was about to receive a new member: 'Before reopening the great campaign, Bonaparte received the submission and explanation of the elector of Saxony, who truly stated that Prussia had forced him to take part in the war. The apology was accepted, and from this time the elector adhered to the league of the Rhine, and was a faithful ally of Napoleon.' Caught in Napoleon's slipstream following the disasters at Jena and Auerstädt, Frederick Augustus, the elector of Saxony, lost no time in deserting the Prussians and hooking up to the French, providing some 20,000 excellent troops. Finally, Napoleon would receive several thousand volunteers from Poles willing to fight for their freedom. They would join General Dabrowski's Polish Legion, which had been fighting as a foreign unit of the French Army since the 1790s. The majority of the Saxons and Poles would serve together from January 1807 in X Corps.

The Campaign Chronicle

———— ◦((•))◦ ————

At 3.00 a.m. on Tuesday, 25 November 1806, Napoleon quits Berlin for Poland. Murat, meanwhile, orders the advance on Warsaw. The French advance is described by historian, A.G. MacDonnell:

'Right up to the end of November the weather had been extraordinarily mild and there had been neither snow nor ice. Snow and ice would have been vastly preferable to the rains. For not even the main road from Posen to Warsaw was paved or ditched at the sides, and when it crossed the innumerable marshes it degenerated into a jumble of un-shaped tree-trunks lying side by side among the reeds. East of Posen the rations grew scarcer, and the capture of a great drove of sucking pigs only gave the men dysentery, and the peasants escaped into the dark forests, driving their cattle before them …'

27–28 November 1806: The Liberators Welcomed

Napoleon arrives at Posen, the half-way point between Berlin and Warsaw. He is preceded by imperial aide-de-camp, Philippe de Ségur:

'The first arrival … of an officer attached to the emperor, and the establishment of his headquarters, which I superintended, had made some sensation there. Attracted as I was by the lively and brilliant intellect, and the patriotic and chivalrous enthusiasm of the nobility of this country, the demonstrative welcome of these ardent and open-hearted souls completely won me. I joined some of their gatherings, where in spite of the seriousness and reserve, which was habitual to all those about Napoleon, I entered into their delight, and sympathized with the hopes of that brave and charming nation, which was so worthy of a better fate.'

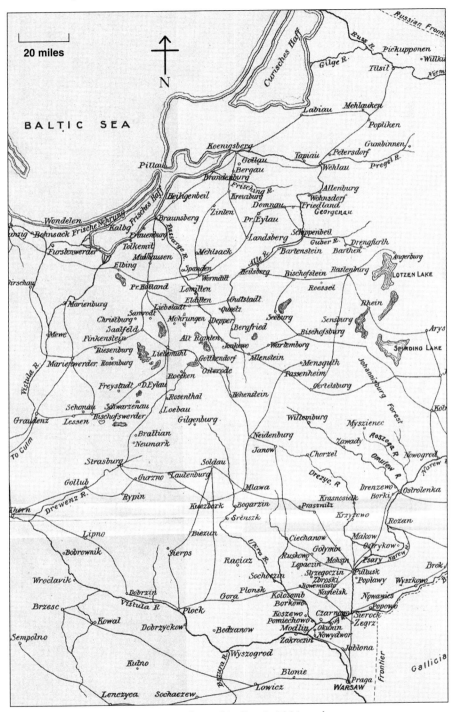

General Theatre of Operations – as depicted in Petre's 1901 study.

Campaign Chronicle

Jérôme Bonaparte (1784–1860). Napoleon's playboy kid brother, in nominal command of the Bavarian and Württemberg troops of IX Corps. According to the Saxon officer, von Funck, Jérôme 'was good-natured, but frivolous and irresponsible, like any other young Frenchman.'

The town is decorated with triumphal arches, illuminations, and signs of welcome, dedicated 'To the restorer of the Polish nation'. But Napoleon – besieged by ebullient town dignitaries requesting the instant reconstitution of the entire Polish kingdom – offers a sober warning: 'speeches and empty wishes are not enough ... what force has overthrown only force can restore ... what has been destroyed for lack of unity only unity can re-establish.' In the evening an icy wind arrives, followed by a downpour of rain: the jolly lamps are extinguished, while the signs of welcome are smudged, quickly becoming illegible.

Meanwhile, Bennigsen – the German-born general in charge of the tsar's First Army – is feeling increasingly isolated at Warsaw, convinced he cannot hold the line of the Vistula against the approaching Grand Army. Consequently, his army quits the suburb of Praga on 28 November and heads north to Pultusk, some 30 miles (48km) distant. Bennigsen's plan is to retreat into the territory between the

27–28 November 1806: The Liberators Welcomed

General Vandamme (1770–1830). The brave and loot-loving commander of IX Corp's Württembergers. A seasoned campaigner, Vandamme was the true force behind Jérôme's campaign against the Prussian-held fortresses of Silesia.

Wkra and Narew rivers, there to link up with Buxhöwden's Second Army, approaching from the east.

As Bennigsen's men trudge north, having retired behind the River Narew, Murat enters Warsaw from the west. He leads his troops into the Polish capital at dusk, resplendent in an outrageously romantic uniform. As at Posen, the French are viewed as liberators and crowds of Polish patriots – no doubt the majority of the city's 100,000 souls – gather to welcome Murat, the grand duke of Berg. Tables are dragged into the streets and squares, food and drink prepared, and Napoleon's health toasted a thousand times. In the words of one citizen, quoted by historian, Christine Sutherland: 'To understand what we felt at the sight of this first handful of warriors, one must have lost everything and hope for everything like ourselves. They suddenly seemed to us like the guarantors of the independence we had been expecting from the hands of the great man, whom nothing could resist.' Meanwhile, according to MacDonnell:

'here was Poland, a fine, historic kingdom, longing for independence and for a real martial king to wield the sword of Jagellon and Sobieski. Murat was frankly entranced with the idea, and the population of Warsaw was frankly entranced with Murat, as he rode into the city at the head of his brilliant squadrons, with his nodding plumes and his gold lace. Prince Poniatowski presented him with the sword of Stephen Bathory, and Murat took it as an omen.'

Murat, the innkeeper's son from La Bastide, was dreaming of a kingdom with which to impress his ambitious wife Caroline, Napoleon's youngest sister ...

2 December 1806: Glogau Falls and Posen Celebrates

The Prussian-held fortress of Glogau, situated some 60 miles (96km) south of Posen, on the River Oder, falls to Bavarian and Württemberg troops serving under Jérôme Bonaparte (Napoleon will soon designate this force 'IX Corps'). Prussian resistance at Glogau collapses with minimal casualties, and the garrison of some 3,000 men marches into captivity.

In Posen, a ball is thrown in Napoleon's honour, marking the anniversary of his coronation as emperor. Napoleon issues a proclamation, flaunting his fighting spirit – 'What right has Russia to hope that she shall hold the balance of destiny in her hand? What right has she to expect she should be placed in so favourable a situation? Shall there be a comparison made between the Russians and us? Are not we and they the soldiers of Austerlitz?' – while demonstrating his desire to dodge the issue of Polish emancipation: 'Shall the Polish throne be re-established, and shall the Great Nation secure for it respect and independence? Shall she recall it to life from the grave? God only, who directs all human affairs, can resolve this great political question.' The Poles of Posen, however, offer up prayers of thanksgiving for their 'deliverance' at Napoleon's hands and sing a *Te Deum* dedicated to their 'liberator'.

But Napoleon has other things on his mind: his soldiers are hungry and the poverty-stricken Poles cannot support them. Requests to buy food from Austrian-controlled Galicia are refused and the situation is desperate. Napoleon can't even procure shoes for his footsore infantry, and as a last resort, requisitions stocks of leather, that the troops might make their own.

Meanwhile, over 150 miles (240km) to the west, Louis Nicholas Davout – Napoleon's 'Iron Marshal' – arrives at Warsaw with the 20,000 men of III Corps. Although these troops have encountered mild weather on their march, they have met with little food or sustenance. Davout's weary troops are hungry but food is scarce. Already the Frenchmen are falling sick as dysentery spreads through their ranks. Nevertheless, Davout marches his men through Warsaw, and after repairing the bridge over the Vistula – burnt by the Prussians according to some, by the Russians according to others – crosses to the suburb of Praga. He plans to force a passage of the River Bug at Okunin, some 20 miles (32km) north-west of Warsaw, but icy waters and a shortage of boats stall the offensive.

7 December 1806: Thorn is Taken and Warsaw Secured

The Grand Army is now across the Vistula, concentrating between Thorn and Warsaw, in readiness to strike Russian positions running north from the River Narew, following the line of the River Wkra. Meanwhile, with news of the fall of Glogau, Napoleon orders Jérôme to press down the River Oder to Breslau, to take this important fort. Poland is peppered with fortified towns, and Napoleon knows that as his army advances, every one of these hostile islands of stone must be taken, otherwise his lines of supply and communication will remain vulnerable.

Still at Posen, Napoleon continues to grapple with the problems of army administration and supply. Although he has some 200,000 troops at his disposal (172,000 infantry and 36,000 cavalry, according to historian, David Chandler), Napoleon does not believe this force adequate to the task. He therefore calls up the conscription class of 1807 early: an unpopular move back in France, where support for the war is lukewarm at best. Meanwhile, to pay for the Polish campaign, Napoleon exacts harsh levies from the conquered Prussian territories. Eventually, he will plunder hundreds of millions of francs from the vanquished Prussians, sowing seeds of hate, which will blossom into a general uprising in years to come. But despite Napoleon's attempts to feed and clothe his army, morale remains low. The French troops – many of whom have been on the march since early October – are reluctant to cross the Vistula and fight through the notorious Polish winter. Extra boots, coats, and bounty are promised: but Poland is the poorest country in Europe and the French troops – used to living off the land – find little of worth to 'liberate'.

In an effort to raise the spirits of his army, and dampen those of his enemies, Napoleon publishes his 40th Bulletin:

'Marshal Ney has passed the Vistula, and entered Thorn on the 6th. He bestows particular encomiums upon Colonel Savary, who, at the head of the 14th Regiment of Infantry, and the grenadiers and *voltigeurs* of the 96th, and the 6th Light Infantry, was the first to pass that river … The Russian Army, commanded by General Bennigsen, has evacuated the Vistula, and seems inclined to bury itself in the interior. Marshal Davout has passed the Vistula, and has established his headquarters before Praga: his advanced posts are on the Bug. The grand duke of Berg remains at Warsaw. The emperor still has his headquarters at Posen.'

Campaign Chronicle

Marshal Lannes (1769–1809). The ferociously brave ex-grenadier in command of V Corps. Wounded at Pultusk in December 1806, Lannes returned in 1807 to play important parts at Danzig, Heilsberg and Friedland.

Meanwhile, the 75-year-old Marshal Kamenskoi arrives to take command of the two Russian armies in Poland, as well as General Lestocq's modest Prussian corps (less than 20,000-strong). As soon as his scattered forces are united, Kamenskoi will have well over 100,000 troops in theatre, and the aged veteran lays plans to take the offensive.

11 December 1806: Passage of the River Bug

But the French strike first. At 6.00 a.m. on 11 December, Davout's troops begin their passage of the icy waters of the River Bug (some accounts refer to this stretch of the Bug as the Narew, with maps showing it as such: but the latter river actually joins the Bug about 20 miles/32km further east, at Sierock), in the face of stiff Russian resistance. Ice floes hamper the crossing, but Davout handles the operation with skill, and manages to gain a foothold on the opposite bank, at the

11 December 1806: Passage of the River Bug

The 'Grumblers' of Napoleon's Imperial Guard on the march in Poland (Raffet).

village of Okunin. The 'Iron Marshal' even manages to push his perimeter a few miles north, to the village of Pomiechowo. Despite a Russian counter-attack, Davout's bridgehead is secure by dusk.

Soon the French presence in the area is bolstered by the arrival of Marshal Augereau's VII Corps, which, having crossed the Vistula just below its junction with the Bug, proceeds to establish a bridgehead. Bennigsen's Russians withdraw from the northern bank of the Bug and occupy the 20-mile (32-km) gap between the Rivers Wkra and Narew. Napoleon summarizes events in his 41st Bulletin:

'On the 11th, at six in the morning, a cannonade was heard on the side of the River Bug. Marshal Davout had ordered General Gauthier to pass that river at the mouth of the Wkra, opposite the village of Okunin. The 25th of the Line and the 89th having passed, were already covered by a bridgehead, and had advanced half a league farther, to the village of Pomiechowo, when a Russian division presented itself, for the purpose of storming the village. Its efforts were useless, and it was repulsed with considerable loss.'

Meanwhile, Napoleon's spies report the roads north-east of Pultusk to be jammed with advancing Russian troops – the 37,000 men of Buxhöwden's Second Army. This leads the emperor to believe a major battle north of Warsaw is imminent. Consequently, he urges Bernadotte's I Corps to Thorn by forced marches, and prepares to leave Posen for the front.

19 December: Napoleon Enters Warsaw

Napoleon enters Warsaw at 1.00 a.m. on 19 December. According to General Rapp, an imperial aide: 'Napoleon was received with enthusiasm. The Poles thought the moment of their resuscitation had arrived, and their wishes were fulfilled. It would be difficult to describe the joy they evinced, and the respect with which they treated us. The French troops, however, were not quite so well pleased; they manifested the greatest repugnance to crossing the Vistula. The idea of want and bad weather inspired them with the greatest aversion to Poland.'

Napoleon expects the Russians to stand firm on the Narew and Passarge rivers, thus denying him control of that area of Prussian Poland between the Bug and the Baltic. But news comes in that Bennigsen is falling back on the approaching troops of Buxhöwden, and Napoleon – eager to keep the two Russian armies apart – decides to launch an attack. His idea is to penetrate the gap between Bennigsen and Buxhöwden, prevent them from uniting, and encircling each one in turn, destroy them individually.

The offensive is planned for 23 December and Napoleon issues instructions to his corps commanders accordingly: Ney's VI Corps, followed by Bernadotte's I Corps, to advance from the Vistula to the Wkra; Augereau's VII Corps to advance some 20 miles (32km) north from its bridgehead to Plonsk, then to turn east and cross the Wkra; Davout's III Corps, supported by Lannes' V Corps, to attack north from the Bug, entering the gap between Bennigsen on the Wkra and Buxhöwden, approaching from the Narew; Soult's IV Corps to march east from the Vistula, in order to link Augereau to the advancing Bernadotte; the Cavalry Reserve – split into two groups under Murat and Bessières – to cover these advances; and the Imperial Guard to remain in possession of Warsaw. Thus, Davout and Lannes are to form Napoleon's right-wing, Augereau and Soult his centre, and Ney and Bernadotte his left-wing. His reserve will be the Imperial Guard at Warsaw.

With Bennigsen's command dispersed between the Wkra and the Narew, Lestocq's far to the north at Lautenburg, and Buxhöwden's still some 50 miles (80km) to the rear at Ostrolenka, a spectacular Napoleonic 'manoeuvre sur les derrières' is in the offing.

Meantime, there is nothing much to do in Warsaw except go to the theatre, as General Rapp describes: 'The French soldiers were particularly fond of passing their jokes at the theatre. One evening, when the curtain was very late of rising,

Marshal Murat, grand duke of Berg (1767–1815). Napoleon's brother-in-law and cavalry supremo, he would save the day at Eylau and lose it at Heilsberg. Ambitious, brave, flamboyant, charismatic, Murat was a great leader but a poor general.

a grenadier, who was among the spectators, became impatient at the delay. "Begin!" he called out, from the further end of the pit; "begin directly or I will not cross the Vistula!'"

23 December: Passage of the River Wkra

Napoleon's offensive is to be launched by elements of Davout's III Corps, with an attack across the Wkra several miles north of its junction with the Bug. The operation is covered by artillery, placed on the heights above Pomiechowo, which lays down a heavy bombardment of Russian positions on the opposite bank.

Campaign Chronicle

Marshal Augereau (1757–1816). The coarse but good-humoured commander of VII Corps. A veteran of the Revolutionary Wars, he was past his best, and led his troops to destruction at Eylau.

Napoleon himself has reconnoitred the area and prepared the plan of attack. The assault is to go in under cover of darkness, spearheaded by General Morand's 1st Division, with Friant's 2nd Division in support: a force of perhaps 8,000 men in all. On the opposite bank the Russian line – consisting of some 15,000 troops under General Count Ostermann-Tolstoi – is extended, stretched too thin to cope with the coming assault, which will be supported by several feints. At 7.00 p.m. a house goes up in a sheet of flame: the signal to attack.

Once across the Wkra, Morand is ordered to storm the village of Czarnowo. The contest is a fierce one, and though the French evict the Russians from the

23 December: Passage of the River Wkra

Marshal Davout (1770–1823). Known as the 'Iron Marshal' for his stern views on discipline, Davout commanded the hard-fighting III Corps, which led the Grand Army's perilous assault across the Wkra in December 1806. Davout's arrival at Eylau in the afternoon of 8 February 1807 dented the Russian left-wing but failed to break it. According to Petre, Davout, 'was probably the ablest of the marshals, both as a strategist and a tactician.'

village, a counter-attack is quickly organized and fighting rages through the night. But Morand holds on and is left in possession of Czarnowo and the surrounding plain. According to F.D. Logan: 'The French troops engaged were said to have been the best in the army; their loss was heavy, especially in officers, but had the attack been made by day, their casualties must have been far more numerous.' In fact, Davout sustains as many as 1,500 casualties; the Russians a similar number, including several hundred taken prisoner. But Davout is across the Wkra and effectively controls its junction with the Bug. The waterways north of Warsaw are now in French hands.

Meanwhile, Napoleon's ADC, Philippe de Ségur, who was present at Czarnowo, laments a sad loss:

> 'My animal had been wounded by a bullet in his chest from which the blood was streaming; and as he could no longer carry me, I had been forced to leave him, loading his equipment on my shoulders. When I had reached our first outpost about 300 paces off, I sat down to rest before the fire, in some grief at the loss of my mount, when a plaintive sound and an unexpected contact caused me to turn my head. It was the poor beast, which had revived, and had dragged itself in the wake of my footsteps: in spite of the distance and the darkness it had succeeded in finding me, and recognizing me by the light of the camp fire, had come up groaning to lay its head on my shoulder. My eyes filled with tears at this last proof of attachment, and I was gently stroking it, when exhausted from the blood it had lost, and its efforts to follow me, in the midst of the men who were as surprised and touched as myself, it fell down, struggled for a moment, and expired.'

24–25 December: Bennigsen Retreats

Amid torrential rain – which transforms the unmetalled Polish roads into rivers of mud – Napoleon's offensive continues. The men of Marshal Augereau's VII Corps, having marched north from the Bug to Plonsk, must now turn east and force a passage over the Wkra, in compliance with Napoleon's orders.

Before them stand the villages of Kolozomb and Sochoczyn, defended by Barclay de Tolly's nine battalions of Russian infantry and five squadrons of cavalry. The operation does not go smoothly, as Augereau's officers recklessly fling their men – and in some cases themselves – across the river, in pursuit of glory. Although Augereau eventually achieves his objective, it is a botch, resulting in unnecessary losses, the first of these being Colonel Savary of the 14th Regiment. Mentioned in Napoleon's 40th Bulletin for his part in the Vistula crossing, Savary – eager, no doubt, for more 'encomiums' – insists on being the first man across the Wkra. Augereau's aide-de-camp, Marbot, describes the crossing and the antics of the top brass:

> 'Augereau … caused General Desjardins' division to attack Kolozomb and General Heudelet's Sochoczyn, directing the former attack in person. The Russians, after burning the existing bridge, had erected a redoubt on the left bank, defended by cannon and a strong force of infantry; but they forgot to destroy a store of timber and planks on the right bank by which we were coming up. Of these materials our sappers adroitly made use to construct a provisional bridge in face of a brisk fire from the enemy, which caused the loss of some men of the 14th of the Line. The planks of the

new bridge, not yet fixed, were swaying under the tread of our soldiers when the colonel of the 14th, M. Savary, brother of the emperor's aide-de-camp, was rash enough to cross on horseback with a view of putting himself at the head of his skirmishers. Hardly had he landed on the opposite bank when a Cossack, galloping out, plunged a lance into his heart and escaped into the woods … The passage of the Wkra was carried, Desjardins' division occupied Sochoczyn, where the enemy had repulsed Heudelet's attack. As, however, one passage was enough, that attack had been quite unnecessary. Nevertheless, General Heudelet, in a fit of senseless pique, gave orders to renew it. He was again repulsed with some thirty men killed or wounded … I have always felt disgusted by this contempt of human life, which at times leads generals to sacrifice their men to their desire of seeing themselves mentioned in dispatches.'

Meanwhile, Davout has consolidated his position with the aid of Lannes and Murat, enabling Napoleon to take possession of Nasielsk, which until recently has been Kamenskoi's headquarters. The French troops (one of whom describes the place as 'a very Jewish town') seek shelter from the rain and sleet, but on entering the deserted houses are appalled at the stench and filth that greets their senses, the Russians having used the downstairs rooms to stable their horses. Mud and muck are everywhere at Nasielsk, as are the corpses and casualties from recent combats. The French surgeons begin treating Russian prisoners, extracting musket balls and performing amputations. The famished troops demand bread and brandy, but none is forthcoming. Supply waggons are stranded miles behind the front. The land is barren. The locals destitute, impoverished. The French – like the Russians before them – take whatever they can find by force. They are desperate: cold, wet, hungry, exhausted. Many are suffering from dysentery or pneumonia. A growing number are reaching the limit of their endurance: a fact graphically expressed by a spate of soldier-suicides.

Next day, 25 December, sees Napoleon on the move again, as he tries to effect the destruction of Bennigsen's First Army. The immediate area of operations constitutes an enclosure or box some 25 miles (40km) square: the bottom, or southern, edge is the River Bug; the left or western edge the Wkra; the right or eastern edge the Narew; with the top or northern edge dry land and thus 'open', accessible to the passage of large armies. Nasielsk marks the approximate centre of the box. With the Russian First Army retreating in a north-easterly direction, the Grand Army's task is to seal the box before Bennigsen escapes or is joined Buxhöwden.

With this in mind, Napoleon makes his arrangements as follows: Lannes (on the extreme right-wing) is to march north up the Narew to Pultusk, with the aim of cutting Bennigsen's line of retreat in that direction; Davout (right-centre), plus

Soult and Murat (centre), are to push north on a broad front from the Bug; Augereau (left-centre) to march north-east from the Wkra; and Ney and Bernadotte (on the extreme left-wing) to continue their south-eastward march from the Vistula, in order to close the 'lid' of the box from the north.

Thus, the French manoeuvres continue, but the swift strike originally envisaged by Napoleon has bogged down, due to foul weather, poor visibility, and horrendous road conditions. Some French infantry units have barely covered 7 miles (12km) in twenty-four hours, while cannon, caissons, and carriages sink in the slough.

26 December: the Battles of Pultusk and Golymin

Bennigsen is already at Pultusk – and Buxhöwden's advanced guard only 12 miles (19km) beyond at Golymin – when Lannes sets his corps in motion at 7.00 a.m. for the final 5-mile (8km) push on his objective. Bad weather has hampered his

General Rapp (1771–1821). Destined for the Church as a youth, Rapp chose the army instead, rising to become one of Napoleon's principal aides. Wounded at Golymin, he would later become governor of Danzig, and would conduct a masterly – though ultimately doomed – defence of the city in 1813, following Napoleon's disastrous Russian campaign.

26 December: the Battles of Pultusk and Golymin

march, and his troops are in a miserable state. Most have spent the previous night in the open, battered by storms of sleet and rain, which have left the roads a muddy morass. It takes an hour for Lannes' infantry to cover the first mile (1.6km) to Pultusk. As for the artillery, it simply gets mired in the mud and Lannes will have to fight the coming battle without it. General Rapp, observing Lannes' difficulties, declares: 'the roads were excessively bad: cavalry, infantry, and artillery stuck in the bogs; and it cost them the utmost difficulty to extricate themselves … Many of our officers stuck in the mud and remained there during the whole of the Battle of Pultusk. They served as marks for the enemy to shoot at.'

The ancient town of Pultusk stands on the edge of the Puszcza Biala (White Forest), on the River Narew, some 32 miles (51km) north of Warsaw. It is held by some 50,000 Russian troops from Bennigsen's First Army (an approximate figure: sources put Bennigsen's strength at anywhere between 36,000, and 68,000). Like their French foes, these soldiers are also cold, hungry and exhausted. Marshal Kamenskoi has ordered Bennigsen to evacuate Pultusk, as there is no food in the area, and Napoleon is known to be advancing in force. But Bennigsen has disobeyed his chief and deployed his men in three lines along a low, crescent-shaped ridge, north of the town. His front extends some 2 miles (3.21km): the right-wing (commanded by the Livonian, Barclay de Tolly) anchored on the northern edge of the ridge, and the left (commanded by the Estonian, Bagavout) on Pultusk itself.

By 11.00 a.m. Lannes arrives before Pultusk and though the 18,000-strong V Corps is outnumbered and unsupported, he launches an immediate attack. Initially, the French assault makes some headway, both against Bennigsen's ridge and the town itself. But without artillery, and with troops already fatigued by lack of sleep and an arduous march, Lannes' strike stalls. The French right-wing is then evicted from Pultusk, and the left shunted off the heights. Thus, as the weather deteriorates, so does Lannes' position: the Russian superiority in numbers and firepower proving too much for French *élan*.

Faced with a severe setback – if not an outright defeat – Lannes is saved by the timely arrival of General d'Aultane some time after 2.00 p.m. D'Aultane is in temporary command of Gudin's 3rd Division, consisting of nine battalions of infantry, eight squadrons of cavalry, plus artillery. The unit is part of Davout's III Corps – toiling north to Golymin on Lannes' left – diverted onto the Pultusk battlefield by the sound of Bennigsen's guns. Emerging on Lannes' left-wing, d'Aultane promptly launches an attack on Bennigsen's right, while fending off a charge by twenty squadrons of Russian cavalry. With French numbers now standing at perhaps 25,000, Lannes orders a general assault: but the Russians stand firm and eventually the French fall back to their start line. A snowstorm is now raging, and as dusk falls the fighting abates, both armies spent and in a state of some confusion.

Campaign Chronicle

During the night, Bennigsen decides to abandon Pultusk after all, and unbeknown to Lannes – wounded in the fighting and running a fever – silently strikes north to Ostrolenka. Left in possession of Pultusk, Lannes – who has sustained at least 4,000 casualties in the battle – will claim a victory. Bennigsen – who lost perhaps 5,000 – will also announce a triumph: declaring he beat 60,000 French troops and blaming Buxhöwden for not marching to his aid.

In truth, the clash at Pultusk was a messy, inconclusive affair. From a purely strategic viewpoint, however, it is difficult to see the battle as a French success, as Lannes failed in the task set him. Not that this was his fault, as F.D. Logan observes: 'The weather undoubtedly exerted a great influence on the operations. It made the roads so heavy that Lannes could only bring up a few guns, and his attack in consequence was sadly handicapped … It was, too, a miscalculation on Napoleon's part in sending Lannes to Pultusk out of reach of support, and in danger of defeat by a superior force.'

Napoleon, as might be expected, plays up Bennigsen's withdrawal, announcing in his 47th Bulletin: 'The engagement was obstinate; after various occurrences, the enemy was completely routed … During the night the enemy beat a retreat, and reached Ostrolenka.'

For an eyewitness account of the fighting at Pultusk, however, we must turn to Thomas Bugeaud, a lieutenant in the 64th Regiment, part of Suchet's 1st Division:

'We were very inferior in numbers, for our forces had not all come up, among them the artillery, as the roads were so bad. However, there was no hesitation to attack, for we are always used to conquer. The chief part of our force was posted on the left, for the enemy threatened to outflank us on that side, thanks to a wood that covered them. On our right we had only three battalions of our brigade, unsupported by any cavalry. With this handful of men we attacked a great line of infantry, protected by several batteries, and supported by a large force of cavalry. Our impetuosity threw them into disorder; they fled on all sides, and the guns would have been in our possession if the deep mud had not prevented our moving speedily. A man could hardly drag his legs out of it. At this moment the cavalry charged our left, which had no time to form, because all the men were stuck in the mud, and could only move very slowly.

'Notwithstanding their terrible fire, the two battalions on the left were overthrown and driven upon the first, where I was. Happily we had time to form square, but we were afraid we should be thrown into disorder by our own comrades in their attempt to escape from death, and we were compelled to kill a good many of them to save the rest, because they were between us and the cavalry. We waited till the mass was within twenty paces of us. Suddenly a fearful discharge confounded and stopped the horsemen – they fell like hail; the rest were seized with a panic, and a shameful flight deprived them of the small share of glory they owed only to the dreadful state of the ground. During our short reverse the enemy's gunners had bravely returned to their pieces, and their infantry had rallied. So we had to encounter a much superior fire. We bore it well, and when we had fired all our cartridges, the officers collected any they could from the killed, and gave them to the men. Hitherto I had been lucky, but a ball came, and struck me just above the left knee. A soldier came and took me by the arm to lead me to the ambulance; but when he had gone a few paces my conductor was killed by a bullet.

'So I was left alone in the mud, and, to add to my misfortunes, some fresh squadrons of cavalry came by the rear of our square, and passed just where I was. I had no resource but to feign death; and they were no more successful in this charge than the first. A man picked me up, and led me to a village, where my wound was dressed. To make the scene more tragic, the house where I was caught fire. I dragged myself as best I could to another quarter, and from there was carried to Warsaw …'

But Pultusk is not the only action fought on 26 December. For 12 miles (19km) to the north-west, a bitter contest erupts at Golymin …

The village of Golymin lies some 18 miles (28km) north of Nasielsk, astride the Ciechanow–Pultusk road, which constitutes the northern edge of Napoleon's operational 'box'. The approaches to the village are covered by woods and marshes, except to the north, where the land rises to form a series of ridges. The ground to the south and west of Golymin is held by the advance guard of Buxhöwden's Second Army, augmented by troops from Doctorov's 7th Division: perhaps some 18,000 men in all (a mean average, as sources vary wildly), commanded by Prince Gallitzin. It is an excellent defensive position, with an escape route running north-east via the Makow road.

The action begins mid-morning, with the arrival of Murat's light cavalry, closely followed by elements of Augereau's VII Corps. The Russians put up a fierce fight, aided by well-placed artillery. But when General Morand's 1st Division arrives – part of Davout's approaching III Corps – the Russians find themselves outnumbered two-to-one. Despite the odds, Gallitzin's little force fights on, gradually driven back on Golymin by increasing French pressure, as General Rapp describes: 'We experienced obstinate resistance on the part of the enemy. He attacked us: we charged with the bayonet; and our battalions drove him back on his own masses. We remained masters of the field: it was covered with the bodies of the dead, and with bags which the Russians had thrown down in order to fly with the greater speed.'

Campaign Chronicle

As the Russian perimeter contracts, Rapp is determined to cut Gallitzin's line of retreat, and a see-saw battle ensues in wooded, waterlogged ground. But as the Russians give way and Rapp's troopers advance, they find themselves bogged down in marshland, serving as targets for marksmen standing waist-deep in the impassable swamp: 'The infantry was dislodged, and the cavalry now advanced. I went forward to meet them and drove them back. But the *voltigeurs*, who were dispersed about in the marshes, overwhelmed us with their balls: I had my left arm broken …'

As at Pultusk, nightfall extinguishes the fight. Both sides have lost around 800 men. Gallitzin is hemmed in to the west, south, and east, but manages, nevertheless, to slip away up the Makow road under cover of darkness. Meanwhile, the French top brass are more concerned with creature comforts, as Augereau's aide-de-camp, Marbot, describes:

> 'Golymin was heaped with dead, wounded and baggage when Marshals Murat and Augereau, accompanied by many generals and their staffs, seeking shelter from the icy rain, established themselves in an immense stable near the town. There, each stretching himself on the dung-heap tried to get warm and to sleep, for we had been on horseback more than twenty hours in this frightful weather – the marshals, the colonels, all the bigwigs in short having, as was right, settled themselves towards the inner end of the stable, so as to be less cold. I, a poor lieutenant, having come in the last, was compelled to lie down close to the doorway, having at best my body sheltered from the rain but exposed to an icy wind, for there were no doors.'

Soon, however, Gallitzin's retreat becomes evident, as the Russians forsake their wounded and at least a portion of their artillery. A scene graphically described by Louis Lejeune, an aide-de-camp (and budding war artist) on the staff of Marshal Berthier:

> 'The Russian loss was very great. The luckless wounded had not the strength to drag themselves out of the mud to join their comrades in retreat, and were ridden down and crushed beneath their own artillery and that of the French in pursuit. No efforts, however strenuous, on the part of the teams of horses could enable them to drag their loads through the quagmire, soaked with blood and made up of the flesh of thousands of victims kneaded with the mire into a revolting mass which clogged the wheels, and the Russians were compelled to abandon all their artillery, including ninety cannon. A great number of prisoners also fell into our hands.'

Bennigsen's Official Report on the Battle of Pultusk

On 26 December 1806 some 50,000 Russians (some sources give 36,000, others as many as 80,000) under Bennigsen occupied the small town of Pultusk, 32 miles (51.4km) north of Warsaw. At around 11.00 a.m. Bennigsen was attacked by Marshal Lannes' V Corps, numbering perhaps 18,000 troops. The French were reinforced in the afternoon by General d'Aultane's division, detached from Davout's III Corps, raising their numbers to perhaps 25,000. The battle set the pattern for future clashes: an inconclusive affair, fought in a blizzard, ending in a Russian retreat, with the French too exhausted to pursue. Meanwhile, 12 miles (19.3km) to the north-east, the advance guard of Buxhöwden's Second Army was fighting for its life against Marshals Murat, Augereau and Davout. Below is Bennigsen's official dispatch to Tsar Alexander, describing events at Pultusk. It indicated a bad case of the 'fog of war' as well as poor communications with Buxhöwden:

'I have the happiness to inform your imperial Majesty that the enemy attacked me yesterday, before 12 o'clock, close to Pultusk, and that I succeeded in checking him at all points. General Suchet, with 15,000 men, commanded the first attack, which was directed on my left against the advanced works of Gurka, in order that they might render themselves masters of that city. I had to oppose them 5,000 men, under the orders of General Bagavout, who defended himself with the utmost bravery, until I could send to his assistance three battalions of reserve to the same point. I also at last detached General Ostermann-Tolstoi with three other battalions, which caused the enemy to be totally beaten on his right wing. The second attack of the enemy (which proved a very sharp one) was directed against my right flank. General Barclay de Tolly was with the advance guard: this wing, on its route to Strzegoczyn, was sheltered by a hedge, in which I had placed a masked battery. Notwithstanding this disposition, the enemy made a feint of turning my flank, which determined me to change my front to the rear on the right: this movement completely succeeded. After having reinforced General Barclay de Tolly with three battalions, ten squadrons, and a train of artillery, the enemy were dislodged from the wood and defeated in every direction: after which they began their retreat.

'The attack commenced at 11 o'clock in the morning, and continued until the close of evening. From the report of the prisoners, the Prince Murat, Davout, and Lannes, commanded against me 50,000 men. All my troops fought with the greatest bravery. The following generals particularly distinguished themselves: Generals Ostermann-Tolstoi, Barclay de Tolly; Prince Dolgorucki, Bagavout, Summow, and Gondorff, of the cavalry. The General Koxin, Colonel de Zéguelin, charged the left wing of the enemy with the regiment of Polish Tartars of Kochawski, and did them considerable mischief. Colonel Knorring, with his regiment of Tartars, almost entirely destroyed a regiment of light horse: and a regiment of cuirassiers, belonging to the emperor, attacked a column of infantry and threw them into the greatest disorder.

'Marshal Kaminskoi departed on the 26th, the morning previous to the attack of Pultusk, for Ostrolenka. He appointed me to the chief command. I was fortunate enough to act singly throughout the whole affair, and to defeat the enemy.

'I regret that the succours, so much desired by General Buxhöwden, did not arrive in time, although it was scarcely distant from me 2 miles in the neighbourhood of Makow, and that it had halted half-way to afford me all the advantages of my victory. I also regret that the absolute want of provisions and forage obliged me to retrograde the whole of my forces towards Rozan, in order to resume them in my rear: what proves how much the enemy must have suffered, is that they made not the slightest attempt to interrupt my rearguard during this movement. I transmit this report to your Imperial Majesty through Captain Wrangen, who was at my side during the whole transaction, and who will acquaint you with every other detail relative to this affair.

'Bennigsen. Rozan, December 26th 1806.'

But Gallitzin has scored a notable success, and one that will earn him praise from Napoleon himself. Heavily outnumbered, the Russian general has used the terrain around Golymin to his advantage, fended off repeated attacks, and marched his men to safety under the noses of some 40,000 Frenchmen. A remarkable feat. Fortunately for him, the weather is too severe, and the roads too bad, for an effective French pursuit.

Thus the actions at Pultusk and Golymin crush Napoleon's hopes of annihilating the Russian armies between the Wkra and Narew. Bennigsen and Buxhöwden follow Kamenskoi's example and beat a hasty retreat out of the trap prepared for them: soon their armies will be safely *en route* for Bialystok, many miles to the east. Away to the north, Lestocq's Prussians are also retreating, out of touch with their Russian allies but still in tact after their eviction from Soldau, courtesy of Marshal Ney. The first round in the great contest is over, but it has been inconclusive, all parties living to fight another day.

27 December 1806–6 January 1807: Winter Quarters

On 27 December a severe frost sets in, adding to the soldiers' misery. Napoleon's army is in a wretched state: thousands sick or wounded and everyone hungry, filthy, exhausted. Food is scarce and supplies of all kinds have dwindled. Used to filling their bellies at the expense of the locals, the French realize they have marched into a muddy desert. The land east of the Vistula simply cannot support

27 December 1806–6 January 1807: Winter Quarters

Marshal Ney (1769 –1815). The fiery commander of VI Corps, whose unauthorized advance in January 1807 is often quoted as an example of his insubordination or his fighting spirit: in fact, he was simply trying to find food for his troops. Ney arrived too late to affect the outcome at Eylau, but played a prominent part in the victory at Friedland.

them. Napoleon estimates that as many as 40 per cent of his soldiers are absent, scouring the countryside for food.

Meanwhile, the Russians are in full retreat, anxious to cover the line of communication with Königsberg, their forward base on the Baltic. But the French pursuit – such as it is – flounders thanks to cruel weather, wretched roads, and a landscape of bogs, lakes and rivers: all of which combine to make rapid manoeuvres impossible.

On 29 December Napoleon visits the battlefield of Golymin, where, according to Lejeune, 'the emperor and Prince Berthier stopped a few minutes to hear us sing airs from the latest operas of Paris.' Napoleon – famously tone-deaf – then presses on to Pultusk, accompanied by the 'grumblers' of his Imperial Guard, including Jean Roch Coignet:

Campaign Chronicle

Marshal Bernadotte (1763–1844). Linked to the Bonaparte clan by marriage, the smooth and scheming commander of I Corps was out of favour for refusing to cooperate with Davout at the Battle of Auerstädt on 14 October 1806. A political rival, Napoleon probably brought him on the Polish expedition to keep him out of mischief. Wounded in the head by a musket ball on 5 June 1807, command of I Corps passed first to Dupont and then to Victor.

'No man could give any idea of our suffering. All our artillery stuck fast in the mud; the heavy guns sank deep into the ground. The emperor's carriage, with him inside, could not be extricated. We were obliged to lead a horse up to the door of the carriage, so that he could get over this terrible place, and go on to Pultusk. And here he saw the desolation among the ranks of his old soldiers, some of whom had blown their brains out. It was here that he called us "grognards", or "grumblers", which name has clung to us ever since, and is now a term of honour.'

On 31 December, Napoleon is forced to accept the Russians have escaped his clutches, and moves his army into winter quarters. The designated cantonments for the various corps are as follows: the Imperial Guard to be stationed in Warsaw; Lannes' V Corps in the Sierock–Warsaw district; Davout's III Corps in Pultusk; Augereau's VII Corps in the Plock–Plonsk district; Soult's IV Corps in the Prasnitz–Makow–Nowiemasto district; Ney's VI Corps in the Soldau–Mlawa–Chorzel district; Bernadotte's I Corps in the Osterode–Marienwerder district. Meanwhile, bridgeheads are to be maintained on the banks of the Vistula and Narew at Thorn, Modlin, Praga, Sierock, and Pultusk.

Next day, 1 January 1807, Napoleon returns to Warsaw, having declared the winter war over. According to Coignet of the Guard: 'When we halted, about 3 miles from Warsaw, we were in a perfect state of starvation: hollow-eyed, sunken-cheeked, and unshaved. We looked like dead men risen from the tomb … The inhabitants of Warsaw received us with open arms … the people could not do too much for us, and the emperor allowed us to rest in this beautiful city. But this short campaign of fourteen days had aged us ten years.'

Back in the capital, Napoleon is again petitioned by the Poles to re-establish their kingdom. According to Bourrienne, Napoleon is: 'besieged by entreaties to re-establish that ancient and heroic kingdom; but he came to no decision, choosing, as was customary with him, to submit to events, that he might the more appear to command them. In fact, Napoleon passed a great part of his time at Warsaw in fêtes and drawing-rooms …' In desperation, the Poles resort to a secret weapon – the youthful and vivacious Countess Marie Walewska – who is persuaded to 'befriend' the emperor for the good of the cause. Napoleon is smitten, and with foul weather keeping the Empress Josephine far away at Mainz, he embarks on an affair destined to change his life and the fate of Europe: though not in the way the Polish patriots hoped.

In spite of the diplomatic and romantic intrigues, however, Napoleon also finds time to visit General Rapp, recovering from the wound he sustained at the Battle of Golymin. According to Rapp the following exchange takes place: '"Well, Rapp," said he, "you are wounded again; and on your unlucky arm too." It was the ninth wound which I had received on my left arm, and the emperor therefore called it my unlucky arm. "No wonder, Sire," said I, "we are always amidst battles." "We shall perhaps have done fighting," he replied, "when we are eighty years old."'

A sentiment shared by the elderly Marshal Kamenskoi, who, though not quite eighty years old, decides warfare Napoleon-style is a young man's game and quits the army. Back at the border town of Grodno, Kamenskoi will strip off in front of the first doctor he finds, point out his old wounds, and demand a certificate declaring his unsuitability for active service. Meanwhile, the combined First and Second Armies are left in the hands of Buxhöwden, the senior general: but not for long. Within days Bennigsen is rewarded for his 'victory' at Pultusk with Kamenskoi's old job. Buxhöwden makes his exit soon

Marie Walewska

Countess Marie Walewska (1789–1817) was perhaps Napoleon's most significant conquest in Poland. Until his liaison with Marie, Napoleon believed himself infertile. The son Marie eventually bore him, on 4 May 1810, clearly illustrated that it was not he who was infertile, but his 'Lucky Star', the Empress Josephine. Napoleon now became intent on founding a dynasty, and divorce soon followed: Josephine being replaced by a fecund Austrian princess. In this way, Poland changed Napoleon's life and the course of European history.

As for Marie, she had married the elderly Count Athenase Walewski at the age of eighteen, bearing him a son in 1805. During the French occupation of Poland, Marie was encouraged to become Napoleon's mistress, in the hope she might influence him to restore the country's independence.

According to a contemporary source, quoted in Louis Cohen's *Napoleonic Anecdotes*, the 22-year-old Marie was: 'fair, with blue eyes, and a skin of dazzling whiteness; she was not tall, but perfectly formed, with an exquisite figure. A slight shadow of melancholy lay on her whole person, and rendered her still more attractive. Recently married to an old nobleman, of bad temper and extremely rigid views, she seemed to Napoleon like a woman who had been sacrificed and who was unhappy at home. This idea increased the passionate interest the emperor felt in her as soon as he saw her.' Napoleon was quickly besotted with Marie, announcing that happiness consisted of a 'bath, supper, and Walewska'. According to Napoleon's valet, Constant, again quoted in Cohen, Napoleon: 'kept Madame Walewska with him at his headquarters at Finkenstein. They took all their meals together. When the emperor was away from her, she occupied herself in reading, or in looking through her window-blinds at the parades and drilling in the courtyard of the castle, where the emperor was often commanding in person. She was an angelic woman.'

And yet, by Marie's own account, she became Napoleon's lover against her will, following the 'the path of bravery' purely for the sake of her country. But she remained faithful to Napoleon until his exile to St Helena in 1815. After this final separation, Marie married Napoleon's distant cousin, Count Philippe-Antoine d'Ornano. She died in childbirth in 1817, her heart being placed in the d'Ornano crypt in Père Lachaise cemetery, while her body was returned to Poland.

The son Marie bore Napoleon – Alexandre Walewski (1810–68) – was accepted by her husband, Count Walewski, bearing his name and title. Alexandre was educated in Poland but fled to France to escape service in the Russian Army, later taking French citizenship. He apparently bore a striking resemblance to Napoleon (though much taller). Under Louis Napoleon's Second Empire, Walewski pursued a diplomatic career, serving as envoy to London. He later became France's foreign minister, a senator, and president of the Assembly. He died of a heart attack at Strasbourg in 1868.

after, to be replaced by the fiery Prince Bagration, who will act as Bennigsen's advance guard commander.

On 6 January, Breslau finally falls to Jérôme's besieging army of Bavarians and Württembergers (now fighting as 'IX Corps'). After thirty-one days the Prussian garrison under General von Thiele capitulates and marches into captivity. Heartened by this development, Napoleon orders sieges of Danzig, Graudenz, and Kolberg to commence. He raises a new 'X Corps' for the task: a medley of Saxon, Polish, French and German troops, some 26,000-strong.

Meanwhile, unknown to Napoleon, Bennigsen's troops are assembling behind the vast Johannisburg Forest, in preparation for a second offensive. Bennigsen's idea is to press forward as far as the Vistula, in an attempt to gain elbow room before the recommencement of major hostilities in the spring. If he can make the Baltic port of Danzig – packed with supplies and threatened by the enemy – so much the better. The move is forced upon him by the fact that his army cannot subsist indefinitely in the Bialystok region. Thus the very nature of the land is driving events, forcing the rival armies to fight over its meagre resources.

10–31 January 1807: The Truce is Broken

And so, with the Russians apparently dismayed after the recent fighting, the Grand Army recuperating in winter quarters, and brother Jérôme's Germans intent on flushing out the remaining Prussian garrisons along the Oder, Napoleon might be forgiven for assuming everything is under control. But events are about to take an unexpected turn: for not only is Bennigsen moving to the attack – silently padding through the Johannisburg Forest – but Marshal Ney has decided to ignore orders and launch a sortie of his own.

Situated some 100 miles (160km) north of Warsaw, the 17,000 troops of Ney's VI Corps are concentrated around Soldau, Mlawa, and Chorzel: only Bernadotte's I Corps – the Grand Army's extreme left-wing – is further north, widely dispersed between the Vistula and the Passarge, above Marienwerder. Like all Grand Army units, VI Corps has received strict orders from imperial headquarters not to advance: the emperor needs a period of calm to prepare for future battles, and the Russians must not be provoked. But Ney's men are starving and on 10 January the headstrong marshal strikes north-east on a major foraging expedition. By 17 January, Ney has reached Heilsberg, some 80 miles (128km) from his base at Soldau: the tempting target of Königsberg – the centre of Prussian resistance and Bennigsen's main supply depot – lies only 40 miles (64km) beyond. At this point, however, Ney is recalled by an enraged Napoleon, who issues a severe reprimand via Marshal Berthier: 'His Majesty orders me to express to you his censure, and indeed regards you as having disobeyed his orders … The emperor, Monsieur le Maréchal, has no need for advice in drawing up his

Campaign Chronicle

General Dabrowski (1755–1818). Having fled to France, following the Third Partition of Poland in 1795, Dabrowski formed a Polish Legion to fight for the Republic. He raised further units during 1806, leading his Polish volunteers at the Siege of Danzig and the Battle of Friedland.

plans: no one knows his thoughts and our duty is to obey.' Ney reluctantly swings back south. And just as well …

For two days later, on 19 January, the cavalry of Ney's advance guard stumbles into that of Bennigsen's, spearheading the drive on Danzig and the line of the Vistula. Suddenly alerted to danger – though not comprehending its magnitude – Ney continues his southward trek to Soldau: but not before warning Bernadotte of the encounter. Bernadotte – isolated to the north and in danger of being pulverized by Bennigsen's advance – is now aware of an imminent threat. He wisely decides to strikes south, in order to keep in touch with Ney and the rest of the Grand Army. On 25 January, however, Bernadotte finds himself embattled at the village of Mohrungen, 15 miles (24km) north of Osterode. Faced by some 10,000 Russians under General Markov, Bernadotte's troops shunt them aside at a cost of 1,000 killed, wounded or captured, and continue south to Lautenburg.

Meanwhile, back in Warsaw, Napoleon receives news of Russian activity in the north, which he immediately blames on Ney's unauthorized hike to Heilsberg. The emperor has difficulty obtaining accurate information, bad weather slowing down communications. But soon, as Russian prisoners bagged by Bernadotte and Ney begin to talk, the scale of the enemy offensive becomes evident. Gradually, Napoleon pieces together a not-altogether-displeasing strategical picture: Bernadotte and Ney – occupying his northern, or left, flank – are in the path of a major Russian offensive, rolling west to the Vistula. But for now, at least, Bennigsen has limited his operations to this northern sector, leaving Grand Army units further south undisturbed: thus the emperor is free to wrest the initiative by launching a counterstroke of his own.

With growing satisfaction, Napoleon realizes the further west Bennigsen moves, the more vulnerable is his line of retreat. He decides to make a massive lunge north from Warsaw to the banks of the River Alle. The plan is simple: to cut off Bennigsen's line of retreat and attack him from the rear. The previous month Napoleon had attempted to destroy the Russians between the Wkra and Narew with a 'manoeuvre sur les derrières' – now he will make a second attempt between the Vistula and the Alle. On 27 January, the Grand Army is galvanized and ordered north by forced marches. Bernadotte and Ney, meanwhile, are instructed to continue falling back, in order to draw the Russians after them. They are to serve as bait for a trap Napoleon plans to spring shut by means of a monster battle of decision.

But Bennigsen's eyes are opened to the coming danger, thanks to a fortunate intelligence coup. On 31 January, a band of Cossacks attached to Bagration's advance guard capture a French messenger near Lautenburg. The rider is one of seven bagged *en route* to Bernadotte from imperial headquarters, but this one – a young and inexperienced officer, fresh from military academy – fails to destroy his dispatches before being taken. Furthermore, the dispatches have not been encoded. Within hours, Bennigsen is in possession of a message from Napoleon to Bernadotte, disclosing French manoeuvres in detail. The Russian commander stops his army in its tracks and orders an immediate retreat on the Alle.

1–7 February 1807: The Manoeuvre on the River Alle

On 1 February, Napoleon continues the strike north, unaware his plans have been discovered. But once again he has failed to take local road and weather conditions into account and the operation is behind schedule. Despite his attempts to push the pace, Napoleon's troops are too widely dispersed – and the Polish roads too few and too foul – to facilitate a rapid concentration. The leading French units make reasonable progress, but the rearward regiments are

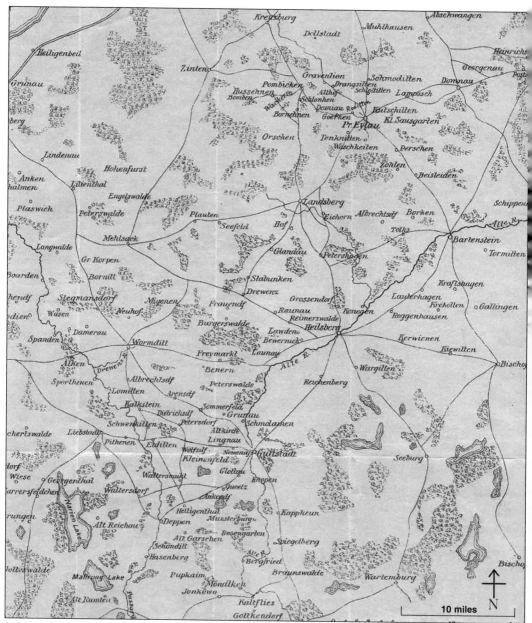

The Theatre of Operations, February–July 1807 – Petre's map of 1901.

left miles behind, floundering in the mud and struggling to catch up. Thus the mesh of Napoleon's net is far too loose, and the emperor in danger of catching nothing.

Next day, 2 February, Napoleon – still believing Bennigsen to be stumbling blindly after Bernadotte – orders a general advance up the Alle to the key

1–7 February 1807: The Manoeuvre on the River Alle

Marie Walewska (1789–1817). Unhappily married to an elderly nobleman, the young countess was encouraged by patriots to form a liaison with Napoleon. The affair contributed little to the Polish cause, but changed the course of Napoleon's life in an unforeseen way.

crossing-point at Allenstein, over 100 miles (161km) north of Warsaw. But icy winds and heavy snow impede progress. The temperature plummets. Napoleon wonders if the Alle is freezing over and thus disappearing – albeit temporarily – as an obstacle to the passage of troops. Eager for news, the emperor flings Murat's cavalry forward. But the reports he receives leave Napoleon dumbfounded. The Russians are 7 miles (11km) north-east of Allenstein, near Bergfried, an alternative crossing-point on the Alle: but they're marching the wrong way. Instead of advancing on the Vistula, Bennigsen's army is retreating on the Alle, and about to disappear over the river and out of reach. With limited manpower at his immediate disposal – five infantry divisions, Murat's Cavalry Reserve, and elements of the Imperial Guard – Napoleon has little choice but to march on Bergfried, in an all-out attempt to catch Bennigsen before he slips away.

Campaign Chronicle

Late in the afternoon of 3 February, some 8,000 French troops descend on Bergfried from the south. The Alle is indeed frozen in this area, but so much snow has fallen that the river can only be passed in the usual manner, by way of the bridge, now in Russian hands. The bulk of Bennigsen's army has already crossed to safety, and the French encounter a rearguard augmented by several guns. The battle begins, but night falls early in Poland at this time of the year, and soon the position is shrouded in darkness. Some 300 Frenchmen are killed or wounded. Napoleon calls off the assault, hoping to finish the business when daylight returns. But Bennigsen evacuates his columns one by one during the bitter cold night, sending them north up the Landsberg road.

Next morning, Napoleon's battlefield is empty. General Lasalle's hussars are sent forward to scour the countryside: they find nothing but roving bands of Cossacks. Once again, the trap has failed to spring shut, and the Russians have marched out of danger. The weather closes in: storms of snow and sleet. The French infantry trudge across the Bergfried bridge and up the Landsberg road, in search of the ultimate battle.

The following day, 5 February, brings more bad news for Napoleon: General Lestocq's Prussian corps – reduced, perhaps, to some 10,000 men – has re-entered the fray, making a sudden appearance on the emperor's left flank. Ney is sent to investigate. His instructions from Napoleon are explicit: Lestocq must not be allowed to link up with Bennigsen. Ney clashes with the Prussians at Waltersdorf and emerges victorious. But the wily Lestocq escapes north – abandoning his rearguard and wounded – and Ney is obliged to follow. Meanwhile, with Davout's III Corps a day's march to the rear, slogging north up the banks of the Alle (having been sent on a wild goose chase to secure the bridges at Heilsberg) and Bernadotte effectively out of the picture, thanks to a breakdown in communication, Napoleon is left with Murat, Soult, Augereau, and the Imperial Guard with which to continue his pursuit of Bennigsen.

On 6 February Murat's cavalry catches up with the Russian rearguard at the village of Hof. As at Bergfried, the Russians are in possession of a small bridge, which is held by several battalions of infantry, protected by cavalry and artillery. According to Murat's biographer, A.H. Atteridge:

> 'Murat had nothing but his horsemen and light artillery in hand; but a few miles away the corps of Soult and Augereau, under the emperor's personal command, were coming up in a long marching column. It would have been common prudence to content himself with merely skirmishing with the enemy, and keeping them under observation till the infantry and field batteries were ready to come into action. But this was not Murat's way. For him "to see the enemy and to charge him, was the same thing." Reckless of the force opposed to him and the strong position it held, he flung his

horsemen into action. Even before his main body had come up, his advanced guard, formed of Colbert's dragoon regiments, was sent struggling through the thawing marshes along the brook, and launched upon the enemy in a reckless charge, from which it came back with many empty saddles …'

Meanwhile, the 1st Cuirassiers arrive on the scene, the leading regiment of d'Hautpoul's heavy cavalry division. The steel-clad cuirassiers form line, breathe their horses, and await orders. General Jean-Joseph d'Hautpoul – a foul-mouthed veteran of some fifty-three summers – arrives to take his place at their head. Atteridge continues:

'Suddenly, like a flash of light and colour, Murat in his brilliant Polish costume came galloping to the front of the cuirassiers. Reining up his horse for a moment, rising in his golden stirrups, and without drawing his sword, he yelled out, "Charge!" pointing with a jewelled riding whip to the enemy's left. Then he spurred forward with d'Hautpoul racing after him, and … led straight for the guns. The storm of the charge burst into and over the batteries, and thundered round the squares on the Russian left. Everything gave way before it.'

Thirty minutes later Napoleon is embracing d'Hautpoul, who, according to the historian, Blond, turns to his troopers and exclaims: 'the emperor is pleased with you … And I am so pleased with you that I kiss all your arses!' But Marbot's description of the aftermath of d'Hautpoul's charge is sombre and poignant:

'The slaughter was fearful; the cuirassiers, furious at the losses sustained by their comrades of the hussars and dragoons, nearly exterminated the eight Russian battalions; all were killed or taken prisoners. The field of battle was a horrible sight. Never was a cavalry charge so completely successful. To testify his satisfaction with the cuirassiers, the emperor embraced their general in presence of the whole division. D'Hautpoul exclaimed, "The only way to show myself worthy of such an honour is to get killed in your Majesty's service." He kept his word, for the next day he died on the battlefield of Eylau. Such were the men of that time.'

The action at Hof is indeed a bloody one: both sides losing over 1,500 men killed, wounded or missing. But despite the slaughter, Bennigsen extricates his army and the Russian retreat continues up the Landsberg road. Meanwhile, according to Jean-Baptiste Barrès, a soldier of the Imperial Guard who arrives later that evening: 'The few houses of the village were full of French wounded.

Their numbers were great, very great, and these were not all, the rest having been left on the battlefield, exposed to all the rigour of that icy day. What a hideous night I spent! Many times I regretted that I was not one of the thousands of corpses that surrounded us.'

By 9.00 a.m. on the following morning, the French advance guard has reached Landsberg, which is defended by troops from Bagration's rearguard. The Russian *Jägers* fend off the French until 11.00 a.m. and then begin a fighting retreat, a number apparently happily drunk on vodka. Nevertheless, Bagration buys time for Bennigsen to press on to the small town of Preussisch-Eylau, some 18 miles (30km) beyond.

Bennigsen has been surprised by the speed of French manoeuvres. When he began his retreat he envisaged a relatively trouble-free march along his line of communication with Königsberg: instead, he has been prodded east with Napoleon's sword at his back. Bennigsen realizes he is running out of options: if he continues hiking east, then he must sacrifice the all-important base of Königsberg; but if he seeks refuge in Königsberg itself, then he will be entrapped and annihilated. Consequently, the decision is taken to turn at bay and make a stand at Eylau.

7 February 1807: Prelude to Battle

Eylau lies some 25 miles (40km) south of Königsberg, a tiny town of some 1,500 souls. It is ringed by a range of heights: to the north is Windmill Hill; to the south a knoll known as the Ziegelhof; to the east a long, low ridge; and to the west a commanding plateau, the so-called Western Heights.

When the first French troops arrive from Landsberg – some time after 2.00 p.m. on 7 February – the Russian dispositions are as follows: the 15,000 troops of Bagration's rearguard are posted on and around the Ziegelhof; Eylau is held by a picket attached to Barclay de Tolly's division; and Bennigsen's main army is concentrating $1^1/_2$ miles (2.5km) away, on the far side of town. An artillery duel erupts. The Russian rearguard fends off successive French attacks, until – overwhelmed by numbers – Bagration is forced to quit his perch on the Ziegelhof and retire through Eylau to the Russian lines beyond. General Yermolov, fighting with Bagration's hard-pressed troops, describes what happens next from the Russian perspective (I am grateful to Jonathan North and Alexander Mikaberidze for the following fragment):

'We enjoyed success for almost two hours, but then the enemy advanced in superior numbers. Of three forward columns, one marched on the main road, where we had fewer infantry, another moved against the Pskov and Sofia Musketeer Regiments and a third advanced against my twenty-four gun battery. The first column moved easily on the main road and

7 February 1807: Prelude to Battle

The Battle of Eylau, 8 February 1807 (contemporary print). The view from the Russian positions with the tiny town church punctuating the horizon. According to Sir Robert Wilson, Russian gunners targeted the church in the hope of killing Napoleon: almost succeeding, they apparently killed 'A favourite mare of Murat's'.

threatened to outflank the strongest point in our positions; the other columns proceeded slowly, due to the deep snow that covered the plain, and had to endure our canister fire for a prolonged time. Although disordered, one of them still managed to reach our positions, where it was destroyed by the bayonets of the Pskov and Sofia Regiments; at the same time, another column scattered its corpses before my battery. Meanwhile, Colonel Degtyarev led the St Petersburg Dragoon Regiment against the column advancing along the main road: to evade our cavalry, this French column veered off the road and moved into deep snow. The rashness of their action led to confusion and our cavalry took advantage of it, capturing one eagle and 500 men, after enduring light enemy musket fire. At least another 500 were killed, including the general who commanded this column.

Campaign Chronicle

The Battle of Eylau, 8 February 1807 (contemporary print). Fighting the elements and each other, over 115,000 men are packed into a snowy space 5 miles square. The picture purports to show Murat's battle-saving charge: eighty squadrons inflicting fearful carnage according to the French; a single regiment of cuirassiers and nothing to worry about according to the Russians.

'I have never witnessed a more decisive cavalry attack. I was equally surprised when I observed how the St Petersburg Regiment quickly descended from a steep snow-covered hill without any disorder. However, our success was short-lived, as the enemy attacked in even larger forces: the French increased their batteries that now covered the movements of their columns, and being unable to contain them, we were ordered to pull back towards the main army. The enemy immediately occupied our positions and followed us closely.

'I successfully carried out orders to cover our troops with my horse artillery guns while they entered Preussisch-Eylau. As soon as I passed the city gates, the enemy brought in its columns and launched assaults on the town, whose defence was entrusted to General Barclay de Tolly, his detachment being reinforced by fresh troops. The imbalanced ratio of forces did not allow us to take full advantage of the walls and fences that surrounded town: the enemy skirmishers appeared on them, fired in the streets, and entered the nearest houses in groups. Our infantry drove them out with bayonets on several occasions and the town was in our hands until gallant General Barclay de Tolly received a serious wound. Discouraged by this loss, his detachment abandoned the town to the enemy and defended only a small section of it. Major General Somov, who commanded a brigade of the 4th Division, arrived with reinforcements, assaulted some houses, annihilated the enemy troops there, and recaptured the town.

'However, Somov made the mistake of rallying his troops in a remote part of the town, and while the drums beat rallying calls, the troops abandoned their positions and did not have time to organize themselves. The appearance of enemy troops spread confusion, further amplified by the darkness and French canister rounds. We had to abandon the town, and in addition to considerable losses in men, we also lost a few artillery pieces. This incident forced the commander-in-chief to change the deployment of our army, and during the night our troops took a different disposition. Bennigsen thought this necessary because the enemy, after it captured the heights defended by our rearguard, made a reconnaissance of our positions.'

According to Augereau's ADC, Marbot, the French assault on Eylau begins without Napoleon's authority, escalating from a Russian raid on the emperor's baggage, into an all-out battle for what little warmth, food and shelter is offered by the town:

'I know that some military writers on this campaign assert that the emperor, not wishing to leave the town in possession of the Russians, gave orders to attack it. I am sure that this is a very great mistake, and I base my assertion on the following facts.

'At the moment when the head of Marshal Augereau's column, coming up by the road from Landsberg, was approaching Ziegelhof, the marshal reached the summit of the plateau, where the emperor already was, and I heard Napoleon say to him, "They wanted me to carry Eylau this evening, but I do not like night fighting; and besides, I do not wish to push my centre too far forward before Davout has come up with the right wing and Ney with the left. I shall await them therefore till tomorrow on this high ground, which can be defended by artillery, and offers an excellent position for our infantry; and when Ney and Davout are in line we can march simultaneously on the enemy." After saying this Napoleon gave orders for his bivouac to be arranged below Ziegelhof, and made his Guard encamp all round. But while the emperor was thus explaining his plans to Marshal Augereau, who highly approved his prudence, the following events were taking place.

'The imperial quartermasters, coming from Landsberg with their baggage and servants, had reached our advanced posts at the entrance of Eylau without anyone having told them to halt near Ziegelhof. These officials, who were accustomed to see the imperial quarters always well guarded, and had not been warned that they were within a few paces of the Russians, thought only of choosing a good lodging for their master, and established themselves in the post-house, where they unpacked their apparatus, and set to work cooking, and stabling their horses. But in the midst of their preparations they were attacked by an enemy's patrol, and would have been captured but for the aid of the detachment of the Guard which always accompanied the emperor's outfit. At the sound of the firing the troops of Marshal Soult, who were posted at the gates of the town, ran up to the rescue of Napoleon's baggage, and found the Russian troops already plundering it. The enemy's generals, thinking that the French wished to take possession of Eylau, sent up reinforcements on their side, so that a bloody engagement took place in the streets of the town, which finally remained in our hands.'

Whether authorized by Napoleon or not, the battle for Eylau abides till midnight, costing each side some 4,000 men. As Yermolov states, Barclay's troops are eventually recalled to the main Russian position, $1\frac{1}{2}$ miles (2.5km) beyond the town. But not all of them make it. A number of Russians barricade themselves in a wooden mill on the edge of town: the French torch it, incinerating the men inside. Meantime, a more fortunate band of fugitives hole up in the town church, where they will remain cornered for almost twenty-four hours, while the storm of battle rages abroad.

Meantime, however, the situation has stabilized. Napoleon with perhaps 45,000 troops is in possession of Eylau, the Ziegelhof and the Western Heights; Bennigsen with some 70,000 (sources vary from 63,000 to 80,000), is encamped on the plain beyond. Both are determined to stand their ground and await reinforcements: Lestocq and Ney being some 12 miles (19km) to the west in the vicinity of Hussehnen; and Davout a mere 10 miles (16km) to the south-east at Bartenstein. Shortly after midnight snow begins to fall – as does the temperature, the thermometer recording 30 degrees of frost – and the soldiers' struggle simplifies into one against a common enemy: cold. According to Raymond de Fezensac, a French staff officer lucky enough to find a billet in town:

'Waggons, troops on foot and mounted troops, the horses, the wounded, the tumult of the inhabitants joined together to create disorder; this was exacerbated by the cold and the heavy snow, and turned the little town into something horrible to behold. I managed to get a place at headquarters. The aides-de-camp were devouring some supper and I managed to pillage a little. Having been ordered to stay at Eylau, I spent the night on a plank with my horse, saddled and bridled, close by.'

As for Bonaparte, he is billeted in the ransacked post-house below the Ziegelhof, at the entrance to town. The crackling of musketry and the doleful boom of distant guns occasionally reach his ears, as sporadic firefights continue to flare up in the streets beyond. But the emperor is exhausted, and without bothering to remove his boots, falls asleep in a chair …

8–9 February 1807: The Battle of Eylau

According to David Chandler, 'None of the great Napoleonic struggles is surrounded with more doubt and uncertainty than the Battle of Eylau … That it was a holocaust, fought under almost impossible weather conditions, all agree, but little else receives unanimous support.' That said, there can be little dispute

The Battle of Eylau, Morning, 8 February 1807 – Wilson's battle plan of 1810. The early fighting at Eylau took place north of the town, when Soult's IV Corps launched a sally against the Russian right-wing.

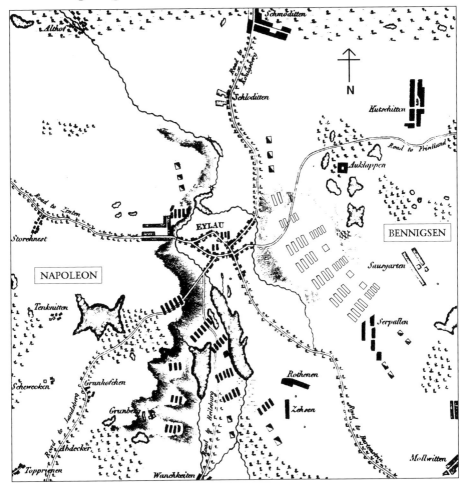

regarding the basic topography of the Eylau battlefield. Enclosing an area some 5 miles (8.04km) square, the killing zone is bisected, roughly speaking, on a north–south axis by the Königsberg–Bartenstein road, and on a west–east axis by the Landsberg– Friedland road: the town of Eylau sitting approximately in the centre. In the north-western sector lie the villages of Althof and Schloditten; and in the north-eastern sector, the villages of Schmoditten, Kutschitten and Anklappen; in the south-eastern sector, lie the villages of Klein Sausgarten, Serpallen and Molwitten; while in the south-western sector, between the Ziegelhof and the Bartenstein road, lies the village of Rothenen. The surrounding countryside – an almost Scandinavian landscape of pine forests, morainal hills and postglacial lakes – is in the grip of an arctic winter, howling into Poland from Russia.

Bennigsen's position cuts across the battlefield in a north-west–south-east diagonal, dominating the Königsberg road, his main line of retreat. The Russian centre, commanded by General Baron Sacken, fronts the village of Anklappen, 1½ miles (2.5km) north-east of Eylau; his right-wing, under General Tutchkov, is anchored on the village of Schloditten; while his left-wing, led by General Count Ostermann-Tolstoi, is fixed on Serpallen. Thus, Bennigsen's host – drawn up in two long lines atop a low ridge – occupies a front of some 3 miles (4.8km), protected by perhaps 460 guns, arranged in two great batteries.

Having summoned Lestocq's outlying Prussian corps, Bennigsen's initial plan is to sit tight till these reinforcements arrive before making his push on Eylau. Considering he already has over twice as many guns as Napoleon and perhaps 25,000 more troops, this seems a passive, unambitious policy: and yet, given the intelligence-vacuum in which both armies are operating – not to mention the atrocious weather, a virtual white-out, which severely hampers all military operations – perhaps an understandable one. Nevertheless, as dawn breaks on 8 February, the initiative lies (whether he knows it or not) with Bennigsen.

As previously noted, Napoleon is in possession of Eylau, the Ziegelhof (the hill to the south of town and the emperor's command post) and the Western Heights. Napoleon's centre – consisting of the Imperial Guard and Murat's Cavalry Reserve – rests on the church and cemetery of Eylau; his right-wing – Augereau's VII Corps, St Hilaire's 1st Division (detached from IV Corps), plus Grouchy's 2nd Dragoon Division and Milhaud's light cavalry brigade – is anchored on the Ziegelhof; while his left-wing – the remainder of Soult's IV Corps plus Lasalle's light cavalry brigade – stretches ½ mile (0.8km) north-west from Eylau to the area dominated by Windmill Hill. Thus, Napoleon's front runs roughly parallel to Bennigsen's, protected by some 200 guns, evenly distributed along the entire line. Meanwhile, a puny reserve remains in rear of Eylau on the Western Heights, covering the Landsberg road, the emperor's line of retreat.

8–9 February 1807: The Battle of Eylau

The Church at Eylau (contemporary print). Napoleon directs an attack (far right) as Russian prisoners are incarcerated in the town church. By the end of the battle, the church was packed with Russians, who lit fires inside to combat the intense cold. In fact, the Russians refused to give up their dead, preferring to lie on the bodies rather than the freezing floor.

Napoleon is outnumbered and knows it. Like Bennigsen, he plans a holding action while awaiting reinforcements. Then, with Davout in place on his right flank and Ney on his left, he plans a double-envelopment of Bennigsen's position, resulting – in theory – in the longed-for battle of annihilation. The question facing Napoleon is: can he hold on long enough? It's a gamble he is willing to take.

Meanwhile, by 7.00 a.m. Lestocq quits Hussehnen in answer to Bennigsen's call. His corps consists of eight or nine battalions of infantry, over thirty squadrons of cavalry, and a couple of horse artillery batteries: and yet, following a series of fatiguing marches, punctuated by frequent clashes with the French, his total force now numbers around 6,000 only. The column is led off into a sallow, sickly sunrise by a handful of hussars and dragoons, supported by a troop of horse artillery. Lestocq is still menaced by Ney, who has posted himself on the general's right, or eastern, flank, with a view to preventing a junction with Bennigsen. Consequently, although Eylau lies some 12 miles (19.3km) due east, the Prussians are obliged to strike north-east for Goercken, via the Forest of Schlautienen, in an attempt to reach Althof and the edge of the Eylau battlefield unmolested.

As for Ney, he has not, as yet, received orders from Napoleon to march on Eylau, and is totally ignorant a major battle is about to be fought there. Even

Campaign Chronicle

when Bennigsen's batteries open up on the Grand Army, the blizzard blows the noise away from Ney, and the marshal remains uninformed. But as soon as Ney's outposts discover Lestocq is on the move, the marshal follows …

It is not certain which side fires the first shot, but by 8.00 a.m. the Battle of Eylau is blazing. A mad scramble ensues in the narrow streets of the town, French troops bolting from their billets to assigned positions along the firing line. The 'grumblers' of Napoleon's Guard are to take post on high ground above the church and cemetery, beyond the southern gate. One of their number, Jean-Baptiste Barrès, describes the tumult as troops frantically try to deploy:

> 'We had hardly slept two hours when day broke and with it a frightful cannonade, directed upon the troops covering the town. Our only thought was to get under arms and out of the town, but the block at the gate was so great, owing to the mass of men of all ranks and all corps who were in bivouac before or around Eylau, that to pass through was practically impossible. All this while spent bullets were increasing the confusion. We reached our post before the regiment received the order to move forward. I had run and struggled so that I was quite out of breath …'

Napoleon, meanwhile, is awoken from his slumber and at last drafts orders recalling Ney. The staff officer, Raymond de Fezensac – who spent the night sleeping on a plank next to his saddled horse – is detailed with delivering the dispatch:

> 'As the first shot was fired the chief of staff ordered me to ride at once to Marshal Ney, inform him of the position of the two armies, and tell him to quit the Kreuzburg road and form up on the left of the army, keeping in touch with Soult. I could not risk falling into enemy hands, nor could I ask for an escort. That would have been useless. An officer was supposed to have a good horse, know all the roads, was never captured or suffered any accidents, always arrived promptly at his destination; so much so that they never bothered to send a second courier.'

Meanwhile, as the sun struggles to pierce the gloom, the landscape is more effectively illuminated by the glow of burning buildings, as the Russian batteries bombard Eylau and the nearby villages. But it is the little church at the centre of Napoleon's position – still full of Russian prisoners from the previous night's fighting – that attracts the most fire. According to Barrès of the Guard:

> 'We were under the fire of a huge battery which was directing against us a withering fire, working terrible havoc in our ranks. Once the file touching

76

me on the right was struck full in the chest; once the file to the left had their right thighs torn off. The shock was so violent that those next to the men struck were thrown down together with the poor wretches who were hit. The order was given to carry the last three to the ambulance post, established in the barns of the suburbs on our left. One of my comrades asked me to help him; he was an old Breton soldier, who was greatly attached to me. I eagerly acceded to his wish and carried him, with three of my comrades, to the house where Dr Larrey was working …'

Dominique-Jean Larrey is perhaps the greatest surgeon of his age. Inventor of the original 'ambulance' – a conveyance designed for the speedy evacuation of battlefield casualties – he is also a noted humanitarian, who insists on the care of friend and foe alike. Attached to the Imperial Guard, he is worshipped by the army as a whole, and Napoleon considers him 'the most virtuous man that I have ever known.' With the battle only an hour old, Larrey's makeshift casualty ward is already filling with broken, blood-stained men, begging for attention:

'While I was operating, or directing operations, I heard on all sides of me the most pressing appeals to me from the sufferers. To the doleful moans of these intrepid soldiers succeeded, after the operation, a prodigious and almost inexplicable calm, along with a kind of internal satisfaction, which they expressed by testimonies of the most lively gratitude. They appeared no longer occupied by their personal evils; they made vows for the preservation of our emperor and the success of our arms; finally, they mutually encouraged each other to bear patiently the different operations which their wounds rendered necessary. It was in the midst of all the obstacles which a hostile locality and a rigorous temperature were presenting, that some of the most delicate and difficult operations were performed successfully.'

Having delivered their burden, Barrès and his companions are faced with a hazardous journey back to their unit: 'To return to the ranks we had to pass through a hail of shot, which struck so close together that one could not go half a dozen steps without being checked by the explosion of a shell or the ricochet of a cannon-ball. In the end I arrived safe and sound, but two of my comrades had fallen dead on the hill.'

Around 9.30 a.m. Napoleon orders Soult to make a demonstration north-west of Eylau, on the extreme left of the French line. With Davout's III Corps approaching Eylau from the opposite direction, the idea is to divert Bennigsen's attention away from the Bartenstein road near Molwitten, Davout's point of entry. Consequently, Soult's infantry advances over the snow towards the Russian lines opposite. Tutchkov, the commander of Bennigsen's right-wing is stung into a counter-attack and a bitter battle ensues. This, of course, is what Napoleon intends. But instead of the prolonged, meat-grinding duel envisaged by the emperor – designed to buy time for the arrival and deployment of III Corps – Soult's attack stalls in the face of sustained Russian aggression. For a few stomach-churning minutes, the battle north of town hangs in the balance: but by 10.00 a.m., Soult's foot soldiers are being shunted back on Eylau, though the bastion of Windmill Hill remains in French hands: 'the battlefield was soon covered with the dead,' records aide-de-camp, Louis Lejeune, 'three hundred cannon on either side pouring out a hail of grape shot at close quarters and working terrible havoc.'

Meanwhile, Davout's steady advance on Eylau via the Bartenstein road continues. But his leading division – Friant's – is intercepted by Russian cavalry as it nears Napoleon's extreme right-wing. Within minutes, Ostermann-Tolstoi's troopers are descending on Friant's advance guard, holding up III Corp's advance, and forewarning Bennigsen of the imminent arrival of powerful French reinforcements. Things are now going from bad to worse for Napoleon: on his left, Soult's hard-pressed troops are barely holding their ground; while Davout's safe arrival on the right has been compromised by Ostermann-Tolstoi's cavalry. In effect, the emperor's army is paralyzed. And all the while snow continues to fall, in the words of Lejeune, 'in such quantities that we could not see two paces before us'.

Originally fighting for time, not ground, by 10.15 a.m. Napoleon is fighting for both. But as the emperor observes, 'ground we can recover, time never.' And so time remains the priority: time for Soult to patch up the shaky left-wing; time for Davout to deploy on the right and stove in Bennigsen's left flank. But options are limited and seconds slipping away. Realizing Davout's deployment is crucial, Napoleon decides to create a major diversion on his right-wing, in order to take the pressure off Friant. He calls for Marshal Augereau.

Pierre François Augereau is a hero of the Revolution: an experienced general, whose coarse good-humour has endeared him to his men. But he is a sick man, and at the age of fifty, past his prime. He has already asked to be relieved of his command on the grounds of ill-health, his plea to Napoleon falling on deaf ears. Now he appears before the emperor with a scarf wrapped round his head, his marshal's cocked hat perched on top. His task is simple: to launch the 9,000 men of VII Corps in a sortie against the Russian left. If at all possible, he is to link up with Davout, battling up the Bartenstein road from the south-east. Augereau's column is to be supported by General St Hilaire's division.

With the snowstorm intensifying into a howling, raging blizzard – cutting visibility, as Lejeune states, to a matter of a few paces – Augereau, leads his troops forward, supported in the saddle by one of his aides. But the French troops are blind and instead of advancing in two compact columns, stumble forward in sections, each one losing contact with its neighbour in the storm. Although St Hilaire's division remains roughly on course, Augereau's corps veers wildly, and instead of crashing into the troops of Ostermann-Tolstoi, walks into a seventy-gun battery supported by infantry and cavalry. The slaughter is fearful: a rich harvest of French lives reaped by Russian roundshot and canister at almost point-blank range. Muskets, bayonets and sabres do the rest, and within fifteen minutes 5,000 casualties go down. And so VII Corps virtually ceases to exist. According to General Yermolov: 'The French stopped in bewilderment at the sudden appearance of our regiments. With a loud guffaw, the Vladimir Musketeer Regiment attacked forcefully and left nobody alive in the French column to mourn the death of comrades.'

Without the support of VII Corps, St Hilaire's puny division is ineffective against Ostermann-Tolstoi's masses, and soon the remnants of both French formations are falling back on Eylau. There, in the cemetery, Augereau – himself wounded in the attack – attempts to rally the survivors. But as Louis Lejeune observes, Augereau's troops, 'left without a leader, suffered horribly: his infantry, drawn up in squares, was positively annihilated where it stood.' One luckless regiment, the 14th of the Line, is stranded in No Man's Land unable to reach safety, and in imminent danger of being cut to pieces by approaching enemies. Augereau sends several aides to order the forlorn 14th to retire, but none get through. Eventually, it falls to Captain Marbot to deliver the marshal's order. Successfully dodging Cossacks – thanks to his extraordinary mare, Lisette – Marbot plunges through the tempest and reaches the doomed regiment:

'I found the 14th formed in square on the top of the hillock, but as the slope was very slight the enemy's cavalry had been able to deliver several charges. These had been vigorously repulsed, and the French, regiment was surrounded by a circle of dead horses and dragoons, which formed a kind of rampart, making the position by this time almost inaccessible to cavalry … Since Colonel Savary's death at the passage of the Wkra, the 14th had been commanded by a major. While I imparted to this officer, under a hail of balls, the order to quit his position and try to rejoin his corps, he pointed out to me that the enemy's artillery had been firing on the 14th for an hour, and had caused it such loss that the handful of soldiers which remained would inevitably be exterminated if they went down into the plain, and that, moreover, there would not be time to prepare to execute such a movement, since a Russian column was marching on him, and was not more than a hundred paces away. "I see no means of saving the regiment," said the major; "return to the emperor, bid him farewell from the 14th of the Line, which has faithfully executed his orders, and bear to him the eagle which he gave us, and which we can defend no longer: it would add too much to the pain of death to see it fall into the hands of the enemy." Then the major handed me his eagle. Saluted for the last time by the glorious fragment of the intrepid regiment with cries of "Vive l'Empereur !" They were going to die for him …

'The infantry eagles were very heavy, and their weight was increased by a stout oak pole on the top of which they were fixed. The length of the pole embarrassed me much, and as the stick without the eagle could not constitute a trophy for the enemy, I resolved with the major's consent to break it and only carry off the eagle. But at the moment when I was leaning forward from my saddle in order to get a better purchase to separate the eagle from the pole, one of the numerous cannon-balls which the Russians were sending at us went through the hinder peak of my hat, less than an inch from my head. The shock was all the more terrible since my hat, being fastened on by a strong leather strap under the chin, offered more resistance to the blow. I seemed to be blotted out of existence, but I did not fall from my horse; blood flowed from my nose, my ears, and even my eyes; nevertheless I still could hear and see, and I preserved all my intellectual faculties, although my limbs were paralyzed to such an extent that I could not move a single finger.

'Meanwhile the column of Russian infantry which we had just perceived was mounting the hill; they were grenadiers wearing mitre-shaped caps with metal ornaments. Soaked with spirits, and in vastly superior numbers, these men hurled themselves furiously on the feeble remains of the unfortunate 14th, whose soldiers had for several days been living only on potatoes and melted snow; that day they had not had time to prepare even this wretched meal. Still our brave Frenchmen made a valiant defence with their bayonets, and when the square had been broken, they held together in groups and sustained the unequal fight for a long time.

'During this terrible struggle several of our men, in order not to be struck from behind, set their backs against my mare's flanks, she, contrary to her practice, remaining perfectly quiet. If I had been able to move I should have urged her to get away from this field of slaughter. But it was absolutely impossible for me to press my legs so as to make the animal I rode understand my wish. My position was the more frightful since, as I have said, I retained the power of sight and thought. Not only were they fighting all round me, which exposed me to bayonet-thrusts, but a Russian officer with a hideous countenance kept making efforts to run me through. As the crowd of combatants prevented him from reaching me, he pointed me out to the soldiers around him, and they, taking me for the commander of the French, as I was the only mounted man, kept firing at me over their comrades' heads, so that bullets were constantly whistling past my ear. One of them would certainly have taken away the small amount of life that was still in me had not a terrible incident led to my escape from the mêlée.

'Among the Frenchmen who had got their flanks against my mare's near flank was a quartermaster-sergeant, whom I knew from having frequently seen him at the marshal's, making copies for him of the "morning states". This man, having been attacked and wounded by several of the enemy, fell under Lisette's belly, and was seizing my leg to pull himself up, when a Russian grenadier, too drunk to stand steady, wishing to finish him by a thrust in the breast, lost his balance, and the point of his bayonet went astray into my cloak, which at that moment was puffed out by the wind. Seeing that I did not fall, the Russian left the sergeant and aimed a great number of blows at me. These were at first fruitless, but one at last reached me, piercing my left arm, and I felt with a kind of horrible pleasure my blood flowing hot. The Russian grenadier with redoubled fury made another thrust at me, but, stumbling with the force which he put into it, drove his bayonet into my mare's thigh. Her ferocious instincts being restored by the pain, she sprang at the Russian, and at one mouthful tore off his nose, lips, eyebrows, and all the skin of his face, making of him a living death's-head, dripping with blood. Then hurling herself with fury among the combatants, kicking and biting, Lisette upset everything that she met on her road. The officer who had made so many attempts to strike me tried to hold her by the bridle; she seized him by his belly, and carrying him off with ease, she bore him out of the crush to the foot of the hillock, where, having torn out his entrails and mashed his body under her feet, she left him dying on the snow. Then, taking the road by which she had come, she made her way at full gallop towards the cemetery of Eylau …'

And it is from the cemetery that the fate of the 14th is witnessed by Jean-Roch Coignet and his comrades of the Imperial Guard: 'to the right, in front of us, the 14th of the Line was cut to pieces; the Russians penetrated their square, and the carnage was terrible.'

And so by 11.15 a.m. Napoleon's position is critical: his left-wing defeated, his right largely destroyed, his reinforcements detained, and enemy troops bearing down on his position. Word reaches the wounded at Larrey's ambulance post that the Russians have actually made it into town, unleashing a howl of despair, followed by a pitiful attempt to flee:

'Already some who were able to march had taken flight; others were making vain efforts to follow them and escape this unexpected attack. We, however, were their prop and support; we were determined to die rather than to seek ignominious safety. I expressed forcibly to all the wounded who remained the resolution which I had taken not to abandon my post; I assured them that, whatever might be the result of this alarm, which to me appeared false, they had nothing to fear for their life. All the members of my own department rallied round me and swore not to abandon me.'

But despite Larrey's cool, the danger is very real, for some 4,000 Russian troops from Tutchkov's command are indeed advancing through the town: many making it as far as the cemetery and the Ziegelhof beyond. This eminence is Napoleon's command post and the soldiers of the imperial escort are obliged to sell their lives dearly in his defence. But within moments the situation is retrieved

A French Surgeon at Eylau

As Napoleon's Organizer of Military Health Services, Pierre François Percy accompanied army surgical teams between 1805–09. Percy was present at the Battle of Eylau, where, like Dominique Larrey (chief surgeon of the Imperial Guard), he was appalled by the numbers of wounded, and the privations they had to bear. Napoleon's surgeons had set up ambulance posts in barns behind the town church. Soldiers had stripped the barn doors for firewood the previous night, so the wind howled through the gaping doorways, freezing wounded and medics alike. Having quit the ambulance post at the height of the battle – in order to catch a glimpse of the action – Percy returned to find it flooded with casualties (I am indebted to Dr Martin Howard, author of *Wellington's Doctors*, for the following translation from Percy's memoirs):

'The noise of the artillery, the smoke of the fires, the smell of the powder, the cries of the wounded on which we operated, all that I saw and heard will never be forgotten … I found the surgical service in the barns full of activity, but what a service! Some amputated legs and arms thrown together with the dead bodies in front of the door; some surgeons covered with blood; some unfortunates with scarcely any straw and shivering with cold! Not a glass of water to give them; nothing to cover them; the wind blowing all parts through the sheds from which the soldiers had removed the doors to make their bivouac close by. I ordered some armfuls of crushed straw to be brought to cover a few of these brave men; the doors of the barn were put back on the side where the north wind blew the most strongly, and having exhorted my colleagues, all around me, to work as long and hard as they could, I returned to the equipment waggons a quarter of a league away. Passing by some ambulance waggons, I made sure that they were giving some soup to the wounded; I arranged for some candles, a new supply of dressings and more instrument cases to be taken to the surgeons.'

by the timely arrival of the grenadiers of the Imperial Guard: 'We shouted "Forward! Hurrah for the emperor!"' records Coignet, 'Our grenadiers fell upon the Russian guard with their bayonets without firing a single shot.'

And yet, if Napoleon has outfaced imminent death or capture, he is still threatened with defeat. The gamble, it seems, has not paid off. But the emperor still has one last throw of the dice, a powerful asset as yet unused: the eighty squadrons of Murat's Cavalry Reserve. According to A.H. Atteridge, Napoleon decided to deploy these horsemen when it became obvious Augereau's assault had failed: 'Murat was beside Napoleon, who with his staff and escort had posted himself on a rising ground near the cemetery of Eylau. Through a lull in the storm the emperor caught sight of Augereau's broken line, and pointing to the Russian attack, said to Murat: "Are you going to let those fellows eat us up?"' Whatever the truth of this assertion, by 11.30 a.m. Napoleon has to act in order to save the battle, and apart from the ultimate reserve of the Imperial Guard, Murat is his only hope.

Thus, by midday, the bulk of the French cavalry – numbering between 10,000 and 18,000 sabres – is drawn up in three lines before Eylau, under a storm of Russian iron and lead. Colonel Lepic of the Mounted Grenadiers of the Guard coolly observes his troopers ducking the incoming shot and shell: 'Heads up! Those are bullets, not turds!' Suddenly, Murat – resplendent in a green Polish coat and fur bonnet, and armed only with a riding crop – gallops across their front, ordering a general advance on the Russian centre. Atteridge continues:

'Six divisions of cavalry were hurled upon the advancing Russians in three successive waves. First came Murat, leading the two divisions of light horse; then Grouchy with the three divisions of dragoons; last, d'Hautpoul at the head of his regiments of cuirassiers. A mass of some 18,000 horsemen rolled down upon the Russian centre, breaking through two successive lines of infantry that had hurriedly formed squares to meet the attack. In the fog of the snowstorm some of the Russian regiments were ridden down before they could form. In other cases squares were broken up. Sixteen standards were taken. The first rush of the charge only stopped when it came upon the third line, the Russian reserve. At this final stage of the attack Napoleon sent Bessières with the mounted grenadiers, and the *chasseurs* of the Guard, his own escort, to Murat's help. This fresh onset broke even the third line, and then the victorious cavalry came riding back. They had disengaged Augereau's beaten infantry, and forced Bennigsen to devote all his energies to reforming his own line, and reduced him for a while to a purely defensive attitude. Murat had successfully charged an army and averted a disaster.'

Campaign Chronicle

It is, perhaps, the greatest charge in history. At a cost of some 2,000 casualties – including the doughty d'Hautpoul, who is mortally wounded and will take six days to die – Murat has achieved his goal and bought a much-needed respite for Napoleon. His monstrous blitz on Bennigsen has relieved the pressure on Soult, Augereau, St Hilaire and Davout. At last, the initiative swings away from the Russians and towards the hard-pressed French. For Napoleon, the crisis is over. This, at least, is the accepted version of events, but one that is pondered over by historian Michael Glover: 'According to French accounts they broke through two lines of Russian infantry, reformed and charged back through the same troops … The Russian accounts … make the event less spectacular and refer to a single regiment of cuirassiers which broke through a gap between two Russian formations … The truth probably lies somewhere between these two versions.' Polish writer, Tomasz Rogacki, suggests Murat attacked with only fifty weak squadrons, including 500 Polish troopers. Rogacki describes not so much a great charge, as a cavalry mêlée, with reserves from both sides being fed in. The result is a series of frantic charges and counter-charges, with the initiative and localized victories swinging back and forth between the two sides. The result of Murat's action, however, is not in doubt: the Russians are thrown on the defensive and obliged to reform their line, as the French consolidate their position at Eylau. A fact testified by surgeon Larrey: 'Calm was re-established, and it became possible for the medical officers to continue uninterruptedly their operations.'

Meanwhile, the 'Iron Marshal' finally makes his appearance on the emperor's right-wing at around 1.00 p.m. The emperor wastes no time in launching him against Ostermann-Tolsoi's open flank, with a drive on the villages of Serpallen and Klein Sausgarten. Davout's III Corps is supported by St Hilaire's division, posted on its left, and linking it to the Grand Army at Eylau. And so, with this new French offensive, the battle swings south, and the Russian left-wing (Napoleon's right) becomes the focal point of the fighting.

But Davout is not the only new arrival on the field. For in the opposite, north-western, corner of the battle zone, Lestocq's Prussians are at last approaching Althof. It has been a day of hard marching and hard fighting for the Prussians, who have slogged their way from Hussehnen through abominable weather and over execrable roads, with Ney's sword at their backs. Some of Lestocq's rear units have been on the march since 3.00 a.m., toiling from Engelswade to Hussehnen in a heroic attempt to catch up with the main body. Nevertheless, the official Prussian narrative makes it sound like a piece of cake: 'Lieutenant General von Lestocq had the fortune to engage Ney's corps, far superior to his, to keep it in awe, to continue his march, and in spite of the circuitous route, to arrive at the field of battle at one o'clock.' Having reached Bennigsen's welcoming arms, Lestocq – whose force has been augmented by swarms of

8–9 February 1807: The Battle of Eylau

Russian stragglers and now stands at around 9,000 – calls a halt: his men requiring a brief respite before being flung into battle …

Meanwhile, Napoleon's dispatch-rider, de Fezensac, has finally found Marshal Ney, after a journey of some six hours: 'I reached Ney at two in the afternoon. He was sorry that I arrived so late but told me that I had tried as hard as I could.' Delayed by bad roads, blizzards, and a self-confessed ignorance of the terrain, de Fezensac's arrival at VI Corps headquarters finally opens Ney's eyes to the unfolding drama at Eylau. Despite his proximity to the battlefield, Ney still has no idea a major battle is being fought: heavy snow and raging winds obliterating the sound of almost 500 guns. The news comes as something of a relief: for so far, the soldiers of VI Corps have had a frustrating, wearisome day, trudging after a pugnacious Prussian rearguard, commanded by Major General von Prittwitz. Now Ney's men are to march to the emperor's aid, and take post on the extreme left of the Grand Army.

Back on the battlefield, Davout's assault seems unstoppable. By 3.30 p.m. III Corps has advanced beyond its initial objectives: Morand's division is north of Serpallen; Gudin's division – having outflanked the forest above Klein Sausgarten – is driving on Anklappen, at the heart of Bennigsen's position; and Friant's division – the extreme right of the advance – is contesting Kutschitten, in the north-eastern sector of the battlefield, a mile (1.6km) in rear of Bennigsen's original front line. Bent back like a hairpin, the Russian left-wing looks set to crack under the pressure, when Lestocq's corps marches into line, stalling the French advance. Half an hour later, with dusk about to fall, Lestocq – by his own account – launches a devastating attack on Friant's division around Kutschitten:

'The infantry advanced now with drums beating, and with such order and resolution, as to leave nothing more to be wished; and without firing a shot, directed itself straight towards the forest, and upon a column of the enemy at least three times their number, until within fifty paces at the utmost. Von Ruchel's regiment, originally led on by Major General von Diericke, inclined to the left, leaving the forest close upon its right, and took post in a diagonal line with the enemy's right flank. Lieutenant Decker's half horse battery took post at the same time on a height somewhat more to the left, from whence he cannonaded not only a ten-gun battery of the enemy's, but also a body of troops posted behind Sausgarten and the forest.

'A brisk and murderous fire now commenced upon the enemy from the artillery and small arms. The Prussian artillery fire was visibly superior to that of the enemy, and the musketry of our infantry, posted in a little valley, caused prodigious destruction amongst the massy body of the enemy, whilst most of his shot flew too high, so that our infantry, in comparison, sustained but little loss. After this tremendous fire had continued for about half an hour, by which the enemy lost, according to his own confession, 4,000 men in killed and wounded, he began to retreat again, and our infantry, till now unbroken, fell upon the enemy with charged bayonets, drove him through the forest to the heights of Little Sausgarten, and obliged him to abandon the farm of Anklappen, which he set on fire, and behind which he took post.

'The setting of night, and the fatigue of the troops, having marched and fought incessantly since 3 o'clock in the morning, made it impossible to pursue our victory further, and to attack the enemy, yet strongly posted in the neighbourhood of Sausgarten, which would have been, no doubt, the cause of the total defeat of his right wing. The general, therefore, having advanced above 2,000 paces, ordered his infantry to mount guard in the forest, and the main body remained on the field of battle, animated with the sweet hopes of effecting the total defeat of the enemy on the next morning, in case he did not retire during the night, and which was the general belief of the Russians.'

Thus, not only has Lestocq bailed-out Bennigsen's left-wing – earning Russian commanders a respite, in order to rally their men – he has also helped evict the French from Anklappen and Kutschitten, driving them back over a mile (1.6km) to the Friedland road.

And so, as the sun sets on the field of Eylau, a curtain falls over the scene of slaughter: an inconclusive affair, in which the two sides have fought each other to a standstill. Although Bennigsen's left-wing has lost territory south of the Friedland road – and now stands at a 90-degree angle to the rest of his front line – it has been bolstered by the arrival of Lestocq and weathered the worst of Davout's attack. Elsewhere, Russian units assume pretty much the same posture they held at daybreak. As for Napoleon, he still holds Eylau – many of his troops having taken time-out from the battle to ransack the town – but despite Davout's arrival, remains at a numerical disadvantage to the Russian host.

But this is redressed by Ney's arrival on the emperor's extreme left around 7.00 p.m. Following Lestocq's route into battle, via Althof, Ney's troops proceed to kick Tutchkov's infantry out of Schloditten – albeit temporarily – before falling into line left of Soult's battered IV Corps. At this point, with both armies fully assembled, stalemate is reached and the fighting fizzles out. Only now, can Larrey and his surgeons finally take some rest, after a shift of some twelve hours: 'Never had there been so hard a day for me; never had my soul been so keenly moved; it had been hardly possible for me to restrain my tears in those moments when I was endeavouring to sustain the courage of my soldier-patients.'

But as night casts its cloak over the terrible tableau, the soldiers of both armies are left wondering which side has won. For the time being, however, there is nothing to do but hunt for food, or like Larrey's surgeons, pass the time, 'on the ice and snow around the fire of the bivouac.'

Bennigsen, however, has had enough. At around 11.00 p.m., with Napoleon dozing in his boots on the Ziegelhof, the Russian general holds a council of war at Anklappen. Physically and mentally exhausted, and shaken by the ferocity of Davout's attack, he considers Ney's arrival the last straw. Thus, in the face of a howl of disgust and indignation from his lieutenants, Bennigsen orders an immediate retreat on Königsberg. A debate ensues, in which Bennigsen is besieged with pleas to stand his ground, many Russian officers believing Napoleon is all but beaten. The general, however, is adamant the army must retire. Consequently, at midnight, the Russians withdraw from the field, covered by darkness and a screen of Cossacks, striking north for Königsberg.

Meanwhile, French nerves are equally taught, with the Grand Army on the brink of decamping to Landsberg. According to Pasquier, Napoleon's councillor of state: 'The outcome of the battle was so uncertain that on both sides, a retreat was ordered during the night.' But at 3.00 a.m., as Pasquier describes, Davout's outposts detect a movement in the Russian camp:

> 'Marshal Davout, who was bivouacking with the most advanced corps, told a person who repeated it to me soon after, that just as he for his part was about to initiate the withdrawal, an officer arrived from the outposts to inform him that a very decided noise could be heard in the enemy bivouac. He then went as far as possible towards the noise, and, on putting his ear to the ground, distinctly recognized a movement of guns and ammunition waggons; and as the reverberation was growing fainter, he could have no doubt that the enemy was in full retreat. When Napoleon was apprised of this, he at once ordered positions to be kept, and that was how the French Army definitely retained the field.'

And so, by remaining in possession of the field of slaughter, Napoleon is able to claim the victory, much to the disgust of Russian generals like Yermolov: 'We soon learned that, during the battle, special orders were issued directing evacuation of hospitals, commissariat and the army treasury. And after this, Napoleon had enough impertinence and brazenness to claim the Battle of Preussisch-Eylau among his victories!' And yet, as Baron Paulin relates, Napoleon has no qualms in claiming a moral victory, loftily declaring to his marshals that: 'When two armies have dealt each other enormous wounds all day long, the field has been won by the side which, armoured in constancy, refuses to quit.'

Bennigsen behaves no better. Having issued the order to evacuate, his next action is to write a despatch to Alexander announcing victory:

Campaign Chronicle

'I am very happy to be able to acquaint your Majesty, that the army which has been entrusted to my command, has been again victorious … Bonaparte this day attacked me with the élite of his troops upon the centre and two wings; but everywhere he was repulsed and beaten. His guards made attempts to pierce my centre, but without the least success, and they were repelled after a very vigorous fire, by charges of the bayonet, and of the cavalry. Several columns of infantry, and regiments of chosen cuirassiers, were destroyed. I shall not fail to lay at the feet of your Majesty, as soon as possible, a detailed relation of the memorable battle of Eylau. I believe our loss exceeds 6,000 men killed, and I certainly do not exaggerate that of the enemy when I estimate it as having greatly exceeded altogether 20,000 men … In vain Bonaparte lavishes all his resources; in vain he tries to animate his soldiers; in vain he sacrifices an immense number; the valour and intrepidity of the Russians opposes itself to all his efforts, and wrests from him a long disputed victory. Master of the field of battle, I remained on it all the night, then meditated upon the part I ought to take, And I cannot but felicitate myself of having moved on Königsberg. It is there that my army, abundantly provided with everything necessary, reposed themselves from their honourable fatigues; whilst the French Army, enfeebled and discouraged, remained constantly upon their arms.'

Napoleon, meanwhile, as head of state and commander-in-chief, has no superior to appease. Thus, as Bennigsen picks up his steps, the emperor picks up his pen and dashes off these few lines to his wife, Josephine: 'the victory is mine, but I have lost many men. The loss of the enemy, which is still more considerable, does not console me. To conclude, I write you these two lines myself, although I am very tired, to tell you that I am well and that I love you. Yours ever, Napoleon.'

'What a massacre! And without a result!' Ney's famous verdict on the bloodletting at Eylau pre-empts those of later pundits, who pronounce the fight a 'drawn match'. At dawn on 9 February, however, Napoleon determines to witness the sequel of the slaughter for himself by making a tour of the battlefield. Among the emperor's party is aide-de-camp, Louis Lejeune:

'Every detail of the struggle, the position of the lines, the squares with the places where the cavalry had charged, were clearly marked upon the ground by heaps of corpses. Many wounded, too numerous for help to be given them at once, had crept close to each other for the sake of warmth, whilst here and there horses wounded to death were dragging their entrails over the snow, piteously neighing to us or to their late riders for help in their

Direction of the Wind at Eylau

The direction of the wind at the Battle of Eylau on 8 February 1807 has remained a topic of controversy. Accounts from both French and Russian sources claim the wind – at times a raging blizzard – blew snow in their faces, severely reducing visibility. As the two armies were drawn up in lines running north-west to south-east, this would suggest the wind was blowing either from the north-east (blowing in French faces) or the south-west (blowing in Russian faces). And yet Marshal Ney, several miles north-west of Eylau, apparently could not hear the sound of the guns, suggesting a north-westerly wind was blowing the sound away from him. The suggestion is supported by General Lestocq, who, marching towards the battle from the north-west, claimed he saw the muzzles of cannon flashing without hearing any sound. Interestingly, Pierre François Percy, Napoleon's senior doctor, talks of a 'north wind' in his account of the battle. Needless to say, a northerly or north-westerly wind could not have blown snow in soldiers faces: except, perhaps, those of Marshal Davout's III Corps, toiling up the Bartenstein road. Did the wind change direction? We will never know.

suffering. I saw one of these poor creatures with but three legs licking the face of his owner, who was standing gazing at his injured steed with an expression of the greatest consternation. He had but a morsel of bread for himself, but he gave it to his horse. The emperor was as grieved as we were at the frightful sufferings he could do so little to relieve … he paused near a group of wounded Russians, whilst his surgeon Yvan dressed their wounds. The Russians, guessing from the respect with which he was treated that he was the tsar of the French, invoked blessings on his head, kissing his foot and stirrups. His whole time was given up now to seeing that the wounded received proper care, and he insisted on the Russians being as well treated as the French.'

Jean-Baptiste Barrès of the Imperial Guard has survived the holocaust, but is overcome by the sights and sounds of universal suffering:

'What a frightful spectacle was offered by this expanse of ground, formerly full of life, where 160,000 men had breathed the air and displayed such courage! The countryside was covered with a dense layer of snow, pierced here and there by the dead, the wounded, and débris of every kind; in all directions the snow was soiled by wide stains of blood, turned yellow by the trampling of men and horses … The wounded of both nations were being removed with the aid of Russian prisoners, which lent a little life to this scene of carnage. Long lines of weapons, of corpses, of wounded men, showed the emplacement of each battalion. In short, no matter where one looked one saw nothing but corpses, and beheld men dragging themselves over the ground; one heard nothing but heartrending cries. I went away horror-struck.'

Another Guardsman, veteran campaigner Jean-Roch Coignet, is also awed by the aftermath, though no doubt heartened by the arrival of alcohol: 'The battlefield was covered with the dead and the wounded; their cries were blended into one great shriek. One can convey no idea of that terrible day ... About noon some casks of brandy, which the Jews brought from Warsaw, arrived, escorted by a company of grenadiers.'

Meanwhile, Eylau is filling up with wounded, as surgeons and stretcher-bearers fetch casualties from the field of battle to the town centre. There is no hospital at Eylau, and as the locals have largely fled, abandoned houses are used instead: badly wounded men are deposited downstairs, the walking wounded led upstairs. Fortunately, the bitter cold has prevented excessive bleeding in many cases, thus limiting infection. But there is little food to go round, the place having been previously ransacked by marauders. On the southern edge of town, the cemetery, as Coignet observes, is 'the burial-place of a great number of French and Russians.' The church, however, has survived: still crammed with some 400 Russian fugitives from the fighting of 7 February. Inside, the men have lit a fire, using benches, the organ, even the altar, for firewood. And still it is freezing: so the shivering soldiers – many of whom are badly wounded – huddle together for warmth. French troops who enter this smoky sanctuary with a little bread for their captives, observe that some Russians are actually embracing corpses.

With both Bennigsen and Napoleon determined to put their own 'spin' on events at Eylau for political reasons, the truth regarding the total number of losses can never be known. According to Bennigsen, the Russians have inflicted some 20,000 casualties on the French, while sustaining 6,000 of their own. According to Napoleon in his 58th and 61st Bulletins, total Russian losses stand at 27,000 (of which the emperor pronounces 7,000 as killed), and total French losses at 6,700 (of which, apparently, a mere 1,000 are fatalities). But historian David Chandler, writing in the 1970s, suggests that in fact, Napoleon's losses exceed 10,000 with Bennigsen's more than double that figure. As the latecomer Lestocq sustained around 1,000 casualties, it seems reasonable to estimate a total loss of 35,000 men killed, wounded and missing in the two-day fight at Eylau. At any rate, the scale of slaughter is such that it will take eight days to bury the dead and remove the wounded.

Murat, meanwhile, leads a lacklustre pursuit: his cavalry trailing behind Bennigsen's troops as they trudge up the Königsberg road. But both sides are sick of butchery and an unofficial peace breaks out, with Murat's men fraternizing with their erstwhile enemies, exchanging brandy for vodka and cigars. Murat assumes the fighting is all but finished, that Bennigsen will abandon Königsberg and march his men home. According to Atteridge: 'A Russian general … shook hands with one of Murat's officers and said the war was over … Some of the Cossack troopers shook hands with the hussars, saluting them by saying "Braves Français!" but they had no more French at their command. There was a tacit truce, and some officers of Russian regular cavalry rode out to fraternize with the Frenchmen.'

10–23 February 1807: The Aftermath of Battle

While Jérôme's Bavarians and Württembergers continue to batter down Prussian fortresses in Silesia, Napoleon – less than 50 miles (80.4km) from the shores of the Baltic – takes stock. Writing to Marshal Duroc at Warsaw, the emperor admits that: 'a very severe battle took place at Eylau. We remained masters of the battlefield; but although the losses on both sides were very heavy, yet my distance from my base renders mine more serious to me.' In fact, Napoleon's army is now minus tens of thousands of men in killed, wounded, sick and 'missing'. Of the latter, a significant number are deserters, scouring the countryside for food. Consequently, Napoleon needs a period of calm to make good his losses by conscription, and is anxious to maintain the 'off the record' armistice with Bennigsen. Thus, the emperor's situation in the immediate aftermath of Eylau is neatly summed up by the Saxon soldier-diplomat, von Funck, who observes: 'Napoleon had, it is true, won a victory by his persistence because he held the field of battle, but was not in a position to exploit it. A victory of sorts, bought at too high a price by the sacrifice of his best troops, may prove quite as decisive as a defeat in turning the issue of the campaign against the victor …'

Meanwhile, by 12 February, the blizzards have abated at Eylau and the temperature rises. Larrey and his fellow-surgeons are still operating, but it is at this point that frostbite and gangrene set in, considerably adding to their workload:

> 'a great number of soldiers of the Guard, and of the line complained of numbness, of tingling or pricking, and of pains in the feet. Those who, while the cold lasted, warmed at the fire of the bivouac the parts diseased, saw the gangrene declare itself there on the commencement of the thaw; those, on the contrary, who rubbed the affected parts with snow, and afterwards with camphorated brandy, were preserved from gangrene.'

Napoleon orders all sick and wounded to be evacuated from Eylau within twenty-four hours: a hopelessly unrealistic request, which in the event will take a further four days to fulfil. Meanwhile, the emperor authorizes the use of every available vehicle – including his own carriage – for the transportation of invalids to Warsaw, some 150 miles (241km) south as the crow flies (the wounded of the Imperial Guard, however, are carried to a nearby château). But despite Napoleon's efforts, there are simply too many casualties for his fleet of carts, carriages and waggons to convey. Consequently, a logistical nightmare ensues, as fights and scuffles break out for places aboard the convoy; and yet, ultimately, to no purpose: for the recent thaw has transformed the roads into a sea of mud, and the makeshift ambulances sink axle-deep in the slough. More fortunate, are those – like the afflicted Marshal Augereau and his aide-de-camp, Captain Marbot – who are seated on sledges, which simply slide over the mud. But for many men – pale, hungry, spotty, racked with fever and diarrhoea – there is no alternative but to walk.

On 16 February, the Imperial Guardsman, Jean-Baptiste Barrès, records:

'Our sojourn at Eylau was becoming miserable; we were without food, and almost without a place to lay our heads, for we were packed on top of one another. The thaw was very pronounced, which made our position even more uncomfortable. At last the signal for withdrawal was announced by a proclamation, which explained why we were advancing no farther and why we were to go into cantonments thirty leagues to the rear. This was only a temporary truce; hostilities would recommence with the fine weather.'

Thus, on 17 February, the Guard quits Eylau at last and withdraws to Osterode, some 50 miles (80.4km) to the south-west. According to Coignet: 'It was a poverty-stricken place. The emperor took up quarters in a barn, but finally found more comfortable lodgings; he was always in our midst, and often lived on food that was given him by his soldiers. But for the soldiers the poor officers would have died of hunger. The inhabitants had buried everything underground in the forests and in their houses. After much searching, we discovered their hiding-places.'

Meanwhile, in Warsaw, the hospitals fill with casualties from the front, as witnessed by von Funck:

'While I was in Warsaw, twenty-seven stationary hospitals had been opened in the barracks and biggest palaces, but they still fell far short of providing accommodation for the ever-increasing number of sick … Napoleon was so weakened by his losses in battle and by sickness in his army that he had to call up all details that could in any way be spared from the fallen fortresses, from Silesia, from Pomerania, and from Lower Saxony. Magdeburg was so denuded of troops that the numbers of prisoners of war exceeded the strength of the garrison by more than four to one.'

10–23 February 1807: The Aftermath of Battle

By 23 February, the bulk of the Grand Army is in winter quarters, established behind the River Passarge in a string of cantonments, stretching from Braunsberg on the Baltic to Warsaw. Bernadotte's I Corps is on the far left, or northern, flank; Soult's IV Corps, Ney's VI Corps and Davout's III Corps occupy the centre; and V Corps – commanded by General Savary in the wounded Lannes' absence – is on the far right, anchored on Warsaw. The Imperial Guard remains in reserve at Osterode.

And so the winter war is over, and Barrès speaks for all, no doubt, with his observation that: 'We had suffered so many privations and undergone such exertions that we might well be permitted to rejoice and hope for a little rest. Moreover, our equipment was in a state of deplorable dilapidation, while our feet were pulp, and our bodies eaten by vermin, of which we could not rid ourselves, as we had no time and no body-linen.'

But while Barrès takes his well-earned breather, battles continue in the Grand Army's rear, with the campaign against enemy fortresses in Silesia and Pomerania. In the former province, Jérôme's IX Corps – having marched south-east from Breslau to subdue Prussian garrisons at Brieg and Schweidnitz – is investing Kosel and Neisse. While in the latter province, Marshal Mortier – aided by a collection of Dutch, French, German and Spanish troops – is besieging the Swedish-held fortress of Stralsund, some 125 miles (201km) north of Berlin.

Napoleon's priority, however, is seizure of the Prussian-held port of Danzig, the so-called 'jewel of the Baltic'. Elements of X Corps, under the command of General Ménard, are closing in, and on 23 February reach the fortified town of Dirschau, some 15 miles (25km) to the south. The town stands on the west bank of the Vistula, commanding the approaches to Danzig, and must be taken at all costs. Spearheading Ménard's advance are Dabrowski's 3,000 Poles: for many, this will be a baptism of fire – as well as an important debut in the fight for freedom.

Dirschau is defended by stout walls, strong gates, two pieces of cannon and perhaps 1,000 Prussians under a certain Major von Both (some sources say over 600, others over 1,500). Dabrowski's solution is simple: artillery. Drawn up in the suburbs close to town, the Polish infantry is thus obliged to shelter from enemy fire, and await the arrival of ordnance. Meantime, in an effort to boost morale, Lieutenant Colonel Sierawski parades up and down in the open, laughing as Prussian marksmen let fly from the windows and loopholes of the town: their bullets apparently peppering the voluminous skirts of his dark blue greatcoat. Half an hour later a lone gun trundles up, much to Sierawski's relief, no doubt. According to Lieutenant Dezydery Chlapowski, a young Polish volunteer: 'At the third shot the gate gave way … We rushed forward and burst into the town, right in amongst the Prussians, who were no longer defending themselves, and we chased them as far as the main square … I later learnt that they had taken shelter with their commander in the church, where they surrendered except for a few who had escaped across the thin ice of the Vistula, but many of these probably drowned.'

Perhaps as many as 300 Prussians escape the six-hour fight at Dirschau, fleeing to nearby Danzig. The rest are killed or wounded: though a party of some 150 men, including Major von Both (who later published a series of articles on the battles of 1806–7), are marched into captivity. This latter group, however, could count themselves lucky, for according to Petre, few prisoners are taken at Dirschau: 'Overwhelmed by numbers, they [the Prussians] were almost entirely destroyed by the Poles, who, exasperated by race hatred, and by the long resistance offered, gave but little quarter.' And yet Dabrowski's casualties are comparatively light: thirty men killed and 230 wounded, the general himself being among the latter. Napoleon is quick to seize on this Polish triumph, and – slightly exaggerating the scale of Dabrowski's success – proceeds to milk it for full propaganda potential: 'General Dabrowski marched against the garrison of Danzig: he fell in with it at Dirschau, overthrew it, made 600 prisoners, took seven pieces of cannon, and pursued it for several leagues. He was wounded with a musket ball. Marshal Lefebvre arrived in the meantime at the head of the X Corps. He had been joined by the Saxons, and marched to invest Danzig …'

28 February–1 June 1807: The Siege of Danzig

An 800-year-old port at the mouth of the Vistula, Danzig is of major strategical importance. A fortified city of great wealth, crammed with bursting storehouses and magazines, it is a bastion on the Baltic: constituting, in Napoleon's mind – as Petre notes – 'a standing menace, whilst in the enemy's hands.' In fact, Napoleon is obsessed with Danzig, considering its capture vital for a variety of reasons: first, to deny the port's facilities to the Russians, who – with the help of the British Royal Navy – might attempt a landing in his rear; second, to remove the threat posed to his left flank by the Prussian garrison; third, to exploit the city's great strategical and material resources himself. And last – but perhaps not least – to divert attention away from his failure to crush Bennigsen at Eylau. Thus, as Petre states: 'Scarcely was the battlefield of Eylau cleared when, on 18 February, Napoleon commenced his arrangements for the siege, which had been interrupted by Bennigsen's advance, necessitating the recall of Lefebvre to guard Thorn.'

Marshal François-Joseph Lefebvre – former commander of the infantry of Napoleon's Old Guard – is, according to Foord, 'merely a rough, honest old soldier of little strategic or tactical ability.' Of humble background (his father was a miller), this tough 52-year-old veteran is a replacement for the unfortunate General Claude Victor, captured while changing horses near Stettin by a party of Prussian soldiers disguised as peasants. Lefebvre knows nothing of siege warfare, but will be aided in his task by Napoleon's top engineer, General Chasseloup-Laubat. As for Lefebvre's command, it consists of the 26,000 troops of X Corps.

28 February–1 June 1807: The Siege of Danzig

General Chasseloup-Laubat (1754–1833). The celebrated engineer who directed French operations at Danzig, Kolberg and Stralsund. At Danzig he was opposed by fellow Frenchman, Bousmard, an engineer whose methods he had studied and absorbed.

Only some 10,000 of these soldiers are French, the rest being an assortment of foreigners, largely Poles and Saxons. But Lefebvre's force will continue to grow over the coming months, strengthened by a steady stream of captured Prussian ordnance from the fallen fortresses of Silesia.

Opposing X Corps is a complement of some 16,000 men, augmented by 450 guns, howitzers and mortars. The bulk of the manpower – around 11,000 men and 300 guns – is concentrated in Danzig itself, the remainder strung out in detachments north of the city, tasked with maintaining communications with the Baltic. Despite later claims (from both sides), these garrison troops are not of the first class: but they are well-supplied and ably led by General Count Friedrich Adolf von Kalkreuth (also spelt 'Kalreuth', 'Kalckreuth' or 'Kalkruth' in contemporary sources), a veteran of the Seven Years War. Like Lefebvre, Kalkreuth is no expert when it comes to sieges, and will rely, in his turn, on an experienced advisor. But this guru is none other than the celebrated French

Polish troops of the Vistula Legion (Job). After the dismemberment of their homeland, many Poles fled to France to enlist. A Polish Legion was formed by the émigré, *Dabrowski, for service in Italy. Thus, according to the Saxon memoirist, von Funck, 'Napoleon had got to know the Poles in his Italian wars and to value them for fine soldiers.'*

émigré, Henri Jean-Baptiste Bousmard, whose treatise on the science of siege warfare, *General Essay on Fortification* (published in the 1790s and dedicated to the king of Prussia) is Chasseloup's bible. Thus, the commanding generals will preside over a game of cat-and-mouse between the 58-year-old Bousmard and the 53-year-old Chasseloup: two clever and resourceful men, seemingly sharing the same textbook. But the game will be a lethal one, and only one of the two Frenchmen will survive.

The venue for the Bousmard v. Chasseloup match is a walled city protected by nineteen bastions. Danzig – an old Hanseatic town – was bagged by Prussia in 1793 during the Second Partition of Poland. The city's inhabitants – Germans and Poles – had enjoyed hundreds of years of municipal autonomy: consequently, Prussian rule was despised. In 1797 a rebellion broke out but was soon crushed, Danzig remaining in Prussian hands.

In 1807, as Petre states: 'the civil population of Danzig numbered about 45,000. The city had somewhat declined in importance of late years, yet was still a very important port and market. Its fortifications had, in 1806, been much neglected, and were in very bad repair. It was only when the Prussian power collapsed, in the autumn of that year, that a siege began to seem probable. Then every effort was made to repair and strengthen the fortress.'

In fact, Danzig's fortifications are formidable, its storehouses full, and its approaches covered by boggy ground and several waterways. It will be a difficult nut for Chasseloup to crack. Above the city, the Vistula – flowing from east to west – hugs the northern flank of the fortress. Then, once past Danzig, the river sweeps north in a wide arc, through a vast swampy plain, known as the Nehrung, before emptying into the Baltic a few miles beyond. The navigable Laake Canal cuts through the eastern Nehrung, connecting Danzig with the estuary, thus creating the garrisoned island of Holm, the southern tip of which gazes across the Vistula at Danzig's northern walls. The mouth of the Vistula is guarded by a small fort at Weichselmunde, opposite the tiny port of Neufahrwasser. Meanwhile, to the east and south of Danzig lies more marshland, intersected by several streams, including the River Mottlau: a tributary of the Vistula, which, running through the centre of the city, bisects it on a north–south axis. To the west – the only practicable line of attack for a hostile army – stand the fortified bastions of the Hagelsberg and the Bischofsberg (armed with forty guns apiece): the first dominating the main approaches to the city; the second forming its south-west corner.

Dabrowski's victory at Dirschau on 23 February has effectively confined Kalkreuth's troops to the precincts of Danzig, leaving Lefebvre free to make his advance on 9 March. The next day, having driven in the Prussian outposts, the marshal occupies villages south and south-west of the city. Several days later, the western suburb of Schidlitz is successfully stormed.

But Napoleon wants Danzig's communications with Weichselmunde and the Baltic cut and orders Lefebvre to encircle the city. Consequently, on 20 March, General Jean-Adam Schramm – operating on Danzig's eastern flank – leads

Campaign Chronicle

Marshal Lefebvre (1755–1820). Replacing the captured General Victor at the head of X Corps, Lefebvre was given the task of taking Danzig. A simple soldier, he grew impatient with his engineers, telling them if they succeeded in knocking a hole in the walls, he would be the first to pass through.

2,000 French troops onto the northern bank of the Vistula, and marches west on Weichselmunde. The small French task force succeeds in pushing the Prussian outposts back along the eastern Nehrung and into the fortress of Weichselmunde itself. Speedily reinforced by Lefebvre, Schramm then beats off a sortie from Danzig, and secures a position on the Nehrung north of Danzig: his right anchored on the Baltic, his left on the Vistula. The French stranglehold on the port is tightening. Now Lefebvre feels himself strong enough to open a regular siege.

By 1807 the basic method for beleaguering a city is well-established. The engineers on both sides know what to expect. First, the attackers will attempt to isolate the garrison by enforcing a blockade. Then, at a safe distance, an initial trench or 'first parallel' will be dug opposite a section of the city walls. Once completed, saps will advance from this trench until a 'second parallel' is completed, and then a third, and so on, until the walls are almost reached. Meanwhile, well-sited batteries will batter the walls facing the trenches, and when a breach is made, the city will be invited to surrender. If the invitation is refused, the attackers will issue from the trenches and storm the breach. Should the fortress fall, a time-honoured tradition – dating back to the Middle Ages – grants victors the 'right' to murder the garrison and plunder the town as 'punishment' for obliging them to suffer casualties by mounting an assault. So much for the theory.

In practice, Chasseloup – aided by his assistant, François Joseph Kirgener – is faced with a difficult task. Danzig is well-stocked, and as long as ships can reach it from the Baltic, the garrison will never starve or run short of ammunition. The city's fortifications are sound, and its approaches covered by both natural and artificial obstacles on three sides. Left with little choice but to attack from the west, Chasseloup bites on granite, selecting the great bastion of the Hagelsberg as the focal point of his campaign. But to keep Kalkreuth and Bousmard off balance, a diversionary operation against the Bischofsberg will also be mounted. It will be dangerous work, especially as the trenches creep closer to the city and come within range of shot and shell hurled from the walls above.

On 2 April the ground has thawed enough for Chasseloup's sappers to start digging opposite the Hagelsberg. This first trench or 'parallel' will eventually run for some 1,300 yards (1,200m). The following day sees a see-saw battle for possession of redoubts west of the city. After a bloody hand-to-hand contest, the garrison keeps control. Meanwhile, the digging continues, hampered by collapsing trenches and Kalkreuth's decision to release dammed floodwaters onto the plain. By 8 April, a second parallel is opened and the sappers are exposed to enemy fire, as well as repeated sorties by the Danzig garrison. In fact, Kalkreuth is conducting a vigorous defence, mounting spoiling attacks on the siege works and disputing every inch of ground. Nevertheless, Chasseloup is determined the trenches must be pushed forward and siege works opposite the Bischofsberg begin. Lefebvre is uneasy about the campaign against the Bischofsberg, which slows the pace of the siege and uses up valuable men and materiél. But Chasseloup is insistent that both forts must be approached, to keep Kalkreuth guessing which one will be assaulted.

On 11 April, the Silesian fortress of Schweidnitz falls to Vandamme and its heavy guns sent north to the besiegers before Danzig. Two days later, Lefebvre receives reinforcements and repulses another sortie by the garrison. By 15 April the second parallel is completed west of Danzig: the besiegers are creeping closer to the city. And to the north, on the Nehrung, French troops under General Gardanne successfully advance along the Laake Canal to cut Kalkreuth's communication with the sea. Meanwhile, staff officer, Louis Lejeune arrives at Lefebvre's camp. Although technically an aide-de-camp to Marshal Berthier,

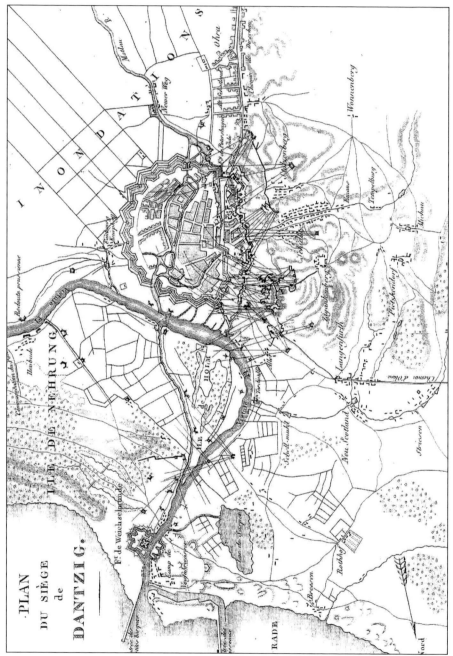

1. The Siege of Danzig. A French map of the siege, indicating the siting of French batteries. Please note the left-hand side of the map is north.

28 February–1 June 1807: The Siege of Danzig

French batteries before Danzig. Some fifty-eight guns shelled Danzig on 22 April 1807, in a twelve-hour bombardment that, if nothing else, caused much psychological damage. The picture purports to show Napoleon inspecting the siege works on 9 May, though according to other sources, he was miles away at Finkenstein, his imperial headquarters. According to Petre, Napoleon sent Bertrand to inspect the works on 5 May, with orders to bring back a detailed report.

Lejeune – a trained engineer – is acting as both a courier and an observer for an impatient Napoleon:

> 'All the best engineer officers of the French Army were collected together under General Chasseloup at the Siege of Danzig, and the operations were conducted with great rapidity, though not fast enough to please the emperor, who, at a distance from the scene of action, did not realize that fresh obstacles were thrown in our way every day by the skill of the directors of the defence.'

On 20 April high winds and snowstorms halt operations before Danzig. But next day, the first big guns arrive at Lefebvre's camp. Two days later, General Jean-Ambrose Lariboisière – commanding the French artillery – orders a twelve-hour bombardment of the city. Fifty-eight heavy guns open up, smashing buildings and igniting fires. Public morale crashes in a storm of panic, as the cannonades continue over successive days. Meanwhile, during the night of 25 April, Chasseloup's engineers complete the third parallel before Danzig's western defences. The besiegers are within musket-shot of the walls and sappers are smashing the palisades of redoubts protecting the city's approaches. Kalkreuth launches a major counter-attack, and when it is repulsed, the Prussian general is invited to surrender. Kalkreuth refuses to capitulate and the bombardments continue. A few days later, General Gardanne takes the island of Holm on Danzig's northern flank, killing or capturing the entire garrison. According to Petre: 'The island was a most valuable prize; it was promptly fortified, and its guns turned against Danzig, the defences of which they took in reverse … The flying bridge connecting Danzig with the island was gallantly cut adrift by a miner named Jacquemart, under a heavy fire.'

But on 10 May, with Danzig encircled and an all-out assault imminent, a fleet of fifty-seven transports appears at the mouth of the Vistula, carrying some 7,000 Russian troops under General Kamenski (spelt 'Kamenskoi' in some sources, but no relation to the ex-commander-in-chief). Kamenski has been sent to save Kalkreuth's skin, his task force sailing from Pillau, near Königsberg, in British ships. Kamenski, so Petre tells us, 'disembarked on the 11th at Neufahrwasser. He was, till he landed, unaware of the loss of the island of Holm, which seriously compromised his plans.' So much so, the Russian general resolves to stay-put and dig-in. This passivity plays into Lefebvre's hands, giving the marshal time to call up Lannes (recovered from his Pultusk wound), at the head of a 15,000-strong 'Reserve Army', which includes Oudinot's élite Grenadier Division.

At 4.00 a.m. on 15 May, Kamenski bestirs himself at last, marching south from Weichselmunde to meet Schramm and Gardanne on the plain north of Danzig. Advancing in four great columns led by Cossacks, Kamenski's troops are in action within the hour, pushing back Frenchmen, Saxons and Poles. Soon after 5.00 a.m. Schramm is hotly engaged and giving ground. Kamenski pushes on, making repeated attacks, the fury of the fight increasing each minute. But just when a Russian breakthrough seems likely, Lannes' leading column arrives to rescue the situation. Outnumbered, Kamenski's force is driven back to the fort of Weichselmunde, leaving some 1,500 dead and wounded on the plain. Kalkreuth's Prussians remain passive spectators, Kamenski's offensive collapsing before effective support can be organized.

And so, with Kamenski's survivors bottled up at Weichselmunde, the siege resumes. Louis Lejeune survives the battle on the Nehrung, but brushes with death on his return to Lefebvre's camp:

'During the battle I rode a horse lent to me by Marshal Lefebvre, and on my way back to headquarters in the evening a ball from Bischofsberg shattered a rock beneath me, and the fragments killed my horse on the spot. I remained flat on my face on the ground for some time before I could get up. The effects of the shock and the pain of my bruises soon went off; I was not really wounded, and I was able to drag myself to headquarters, where the rejoicings over the victory soon quite restored me.'

Several days later, Lejeune describes the scene when a British corvette, the *Dauntless*, enters the Vistula, and sailing past Weichselmunde, attempts to deliver supplies to Kalkreuth's incarcerated garrison:

'on 19 May an English sloop of war with twenty-four guns tried to run the blockade and get into the town by way of an arm of the Vistula which winds through the meadows round Danzig. The bold commander of the vessel hoped to break down every obstacle with discharges of grape shot from his cannon. He had actually got within range of the town, having met with no more formidable obstacles than a few simple booms, which were easily broken through. He was not, however, prepared for the sudden attack opened upon him by several companies of our sharpshooters, who rushed across the meadows and fired a volley into the ship from both sides of the stream, mowing down the sailors and bringing the sloop to a standstill. Without helmsmen, and with sails flapping helplessly, the vessel drifted to the side of the stream and grounded; the soldiers sprang on board and took 150 prisoners as well as the valuable cargo of weapons, ammunition, and provisions which the commander had intended for the use of the garrison of the beleaguered city.'

Cut off from the sea, the Danzig garrison is doomed, and on 20 May Kalkreuth opens tentative peace negotiations. He is offered honourable, even generous, terms by Lefebvre – a sign, perhaps, of Napoleon's need to close the siege quickly – including the right to march his garrison out of the city, 'with arms and bag-gage, drums beating, colours flying, matches lighted, with two pieces of light artillery, six pounders, and their ammunition waggons, each drawn by six horses.' Furthermore, a safe passage is guaranteed to Kalkreuth's officers, on condition they swear not to bear arms against France for twelve months from the date of surrender. Kalkreuth signs, but inserts a clause stipulating that capitulation will only come into effect if the city is not relieved by noon on 26 May.

But Lefebvre – running out of patience and fearful of another Allied attempt to relieve the city – decides to storm Danzig as soon as possible, as described by Louis Lejeune:

'Marshal Lefebvre was as impatient as we were to get into the town and to put an end to the tedious operations … One day the marshal, angry at all the delays, took me by the arm and began banging with his fist at the base of a wall, pierced by the sap, shouting in his Alsatian brogue, "Make a hole here, and I'll be the first to go through it." Meanwhile the walls were falling under our bombardment, and a practicable breach had at last just been made. Troops were ready for the assault, and the decisive blow was to be struck the next morning …'

On 23 May, however, events take an unexpected turn: Kamenski's Russians re-embark at Weichselmunde and sail back to Pillau, while the ethnic Poles among the Prussian garrison start to desert. Then, Danzig's shopkeepers appear at the city gates, setting up stalls and selling wine to Lefebvre's troops at thirty-two *sous* a bottle. It is clear everyone is sick of the siege. Soon the soldiers of both sides are fraternizing, merrily getting drunk together. Finally, the arrival of Marshal Mortier with a further 12,000 French troops decides the issue and Kalkreuth announces his desire to quit. Thus, Danzig is spared the trauma of a bloody assault, and on 27 May the defenders march out and the besiegers march in, led by Chasseloup's sappers.

In his official report to Frederick William, Kalkreuth blames mass desertion for the fall of Danzig: though it is only after the capitulation that large numbers – some 2,000 Pomeranian Poles forced to fight for Prussia – go over to the French. But it is reasonable to assume that falling morale – rather than dwindling numbers or supplies – is a factor in the Prussian surrender, as Petre notes:

'From famine or shortness of supplies or ammunition the garrison had never suffered. Enormous quantities of stores of every description remained in the place, and were of the utmost service to the French. Whether Kalkreuth should not have held out longer is a moot point. The Hagelsberg would probably have been stormed with great slaughter on both sides …'

And so, despite orders from Frederick William to defend Danzig to the last, Kalkreuth opts to save lives by capitulating in the face of lengthening odds. He has lost some 3,000 men during the siege from sickness and enemy action. Among the dead is engineer Bousmard, killed by his own countrymen. But Kalkreuth is not disgraced, the Prussian king quickly promoting him to field marshal. Equally gratifying – perhaps more so – is public praise from Napoleon, who considers Kalkreuth's defence of Danzig masterly.

But then, Napoleon could afford to be generous to his enemies. In fact, with Danzig's coffers at his mercy, he could afford to be generous to everyone, each soldier of X Corps being awarded a bonus of 10 francs. Lefebvre, meanwhile, is sent a box of chocolates. The gruff marshal – perhaps baffled at first – is delighted to find 300 banknotes inside, each of 1,000 francs denomination (according to Blond, soldiers will refer to cash as 'Danzig chocolate' for years to

Dazing Capitulates: Terms of Surrender

Danzig fell on 27 May 1807 but terms for its surrender had been negotiated seven days before. The document made provision for a Prussian surrender if the garrison had not been relieved by noon on the 26th. The terms granted the garrison are generally regarded as fair, if not generous: indication of Napoleon's desire to bring the siege to a successful conclusion as quickly as possible:

Article I. The garrison shall march out on the morning of the 27th, with arms and baggage, drums beating, colours flying, matches lighted, with two pieces of light artillery, six pounders, and their ammunition waggons, each drawn by six horses.

II. The remainder of the artillery horses shall be delivered up to the French.

III. All the arms, of every kind, beyond what may be necessary for the officers and troops who leave the place, shall be delivered up to the officers of artillery nominated for that purpose.

IV. The garrison shall be conducted to the advanced posts of the army of his Prussian Majesty at Pillau, passing through the Nehrung; and night quarters shall be assigned them for a march of five days.

V. The garrison engages not to act against the French Army or its allies, during one year, from the day of signing the capitulation. General Count Kalkreuth, his Highness Prince Scherbatow, and the rest of the officers, engage, upon their honour, to observe, and cause the present article to be observed.

VI. Hagelsberg, and the gates of Oliva, Jacob, and Neugarten, shall be delivered up to the troops of his Majesty the emperor and king, and those of his allies, on the 26th, at noon.

VII. The officers, subalterns, and privates, at present prisoners in Danzig, whether belonging to his Majesty the emperor, or his allies, shall be liberated without being ex-changed.

VIII. In order to prevent confusion, the troops of his Majesty the emperor, and those of his allies, shall not enter Danzig till the Prussians and Russians have withdrawn. However, a piquet shall be admitted into the place, and guards be posted at the gates.

IX. As the means of conveying the whole baggage out of the place are not sufficient, a vessel shall be granted to sail directly for Pillau. The freighting of this vessel shall be made in the presence of a French officer, nominated for this purpose.

X. Officers of the engineers and artillery shall be nominated on both sides, to take charge of what relates to the army, not forgetting the plans, charts, etc.

XI. The magazines, regimental chests, and every thing in general, belonging to the king, shall be given up to the French administration, and a commissary shall be nominated to deliver them to the person provided with full powers to receive them by His Excellency Marshal Lefebvre.

XII. The Prussian Officers, prisoners on parole, who were with their families in Danzig before the blockade commenced, may remain there, waiting for fresh orders from His Excellency the Prince of Neufchâtel, major general; nevertheless, to enjoy this advantage, it will be necessary for them to produce a certificate, to attest that they have not taken any part in the defence of the place.

XIII. All the women belonging to the officers, and others, or persons in a civil employ, shall be free to leave the place, and shall have passports granted them.

XIV. The sick and wounded shall be left to the generosity of His Excellency Marshal Lefebvre; officers and surgeons shall be left to take care of them, to preserve good order and provide necessaries. As soon as they recover, they shall be sent to the advanced posts of the Prussian Army, and enjoy the privileges of the capitulation.

XV. An accurate list of the officers, subalterns, and privates of each regiment, shall be delivered to His Excellency Marshal Lefebvre. The military remaining in the hospitals shall be inscribed in a separate list.

XVI. His Excellency Marshal Lefebvre has assured the inhabitants of Danzig that he will use every means to cause persons and property to be respected; and that the best order shall be maintained in the garrison.

XVII. A superior officer shall be sent to the respective headquarters to guarantee the execution of the capitulation.

XVIII. The present capitulation shall be carried into execution, if, by the 26th at noon, the garrison shall not have been relieved. It is understood that from the present time till then, the garrison of Danzig shall not make any attack upon the besiegers, supposing any engagement should take place in the vicinity of the place.

Done at Danzig, 20 May 1807.
(Signed) The General of Cavalry,
Kalkreuth, Governor.

come). A year later, Napoleon will make Lefevbre duke of Danzig, with a gratuity of two and a half millions. Meanwhile, having scored a major military, political and financial coup at the cost of some 6,000 men (1,500 of them Poles), a gleeful Napoleon announces the fall of Danzig in his 67th Bulletin of 29 May 1807: 'Danzig has capitulated. That fine city is in our possession. Eight hundred pieces of artillery, magazines of every kind, more than 500,000 quintals of grain, well-stored cellars, immense collections of clothing and spices; great resources of every kind for the army … Marshal Lefebvre has braved all; he has animated with

28 February–1 June 1807: The Siege of Danzig

Marshal Mortier (1768–1835). The half-English commander of VIII Corps, which spent much of the campaign in Pomerania. Nevertheless, Mortier led Napoleon's left-wing at Friedland.

the same spirit the Saxons, the Poles, the troops of Baden, and has made them all conduce to his end.'

On 31 May, Napoleon visits Danzig with General Rapp, the new military governor. This is a fact finding mission, aimed at discovering the city's resources and how best to exploit them. The following day, the emperor attends a banquet at the grand town hall. The feast is thrown by the city fathers in his honour, but the emperor graces the occasion for little more than an hour. Meanwhile, despite Article XVI of the terms of surrender – guaranteeing that property will be respected and order maintained – Danzig is suffering at the hands of the victorious soldiery. Despite the pleas of the citizens, which go unheard, Napoleon's troops seize food, steal art treasures, and publicly burn all English goods. But Danzig's despoliation does not stop here. All French troops – some 10,000 – are to be billeted at the city's expense, and a sum of 20 million francs given up to the emperor. Unable to raise this mountain of cash – even by a harsh levy on the population – Danzig's authorities resort to issuing paper money, thus

The Sieges of Pomerania and Silesia

'The fall of Danzig and the coming of spring made a profound difference to the material and moral condition of the Grande Armée,' writes historian, A.G. MacDonnell. Yet the siege was just one of several assaults on Prussian-held fortresses behind the French front line. When Danzig fell, therefore, other sieges were continuing at Graudenz, Kolberg, Stralsund, and the Silesian fortresses of Kosel and Neisse (Breslau, Schweidnitz and Brieg having already fallen).

At Graudenz, the siege began on 22 January and was destined to last until 9 July, when hostilities formally ended. Standing some 60 miles (96.5km) south of Danzig, Graudenz was a fortified inland port on the banks of the Vistula. General Rouyer opened the siege for Napoleon, but was replaced by General Victor in May, following the latter's release from captivity. The besieging troops, detached from Marshal Lefebvre's X Corps – Germans from Hesse–Darmstadt and Poles from Dabrowski's 1st Legion of the North – numbered some 7,000. Holding the city (founded by the Teutonic Knights in the thirteenth century, and boasting a Gothic church and a Jesuit college) was 73-year-old General L'Homme de Courbière with a garrison of 4,500. Despite a steady stream of deserters – ethnic Poles eager to escape Prussian rule – the garrison held out against long odds, till the Treaty of Tilsit brought an end to the war.

Similarly, at Kolberg – roughly 100 miles (160.9km) west of Danzig – the Prussian garrison grimly clung on till the arrival of peace. The siege began in mid-March 1807, when the Baltic port attracted the attention of Marshal Mortier, leading 14,000 troops from VIII Corps. But the garrison – 6,000 men under General Augustus Wilhelm Graf Neithard von Gneisenau – conducted a spirited defence, launching many sorties. The desperate nature of the conflict was reflected in the casualty rates, both sides' losses pushing 50 per cent: though many succumbed to fever. Gneisenau emerged from Kolberg a national hero, and in a letter to the Swedish king, dated 18 June 1807 (quoted by Wilson), the general gives some idea of his garrison's ordeal, and its fighting spirit:

'I had in haste raised a small field fortification on the Wolfsberg, situated about 2,000 paces from the fortress, which the enemy had already twice attacked, and twice been repulsed with considerable loss. He then began to lay a regular siege to it, completed the first and second parallels, and made mines under the protection of ten redoubts. More than 7,000 shot had already been fired, when on 11 June, the enemy's batteries began to play on the above fortification, and made a breach … having filled his trenches with troops, he summoned the Wolfsberg, which was half destroyed, and effected a kind of capitulation, which was accepted. All the artillery was removed, and thus the enemy obtained possession of that small fortification after ten days' siege. Since that time we have made two vigorous sorties, in one of which we retook the Wolfsberg in a few minutes, which had cost the enemy a regular siege. In these two sallies the enemy had upwards of 2,000 men killed and wounded, one howitzer was taken, six pieces of cannon spiked, and nearly a whole battalion made prisoners, among whom were one colonel, one lieutenant colonel, two captains, and six lieutenants …'

Around 100 miles (160.9km) west of Kolberg, the ancient port of Stralsund was invested in late January 1807. The city and its environs were pretty much all that remained of Swedish Pomerania, a Medieval relic much eroded by Prussia's territorial gains of the eighteenth century. The Swedish king, Gustavus IV, had declared against Napoleon following the duc d'Enghien's execution in 1804. The upshot – a belated and botched campaign in support of the Third Coalition – quickly saw 15,000 Swedes bottled up behind Stralsund's Medieval gates, under the command of General Jean Henri Essen. Marshal Mortier – Napoleon's so-called 'Big Mortar' – arrived before the port and throughout February and March, the sappers of VIII Corps dug trenches and scuffled with Essen's Swedes, whose firepower was augmented by Baltic gunboats. On 29 March, Mortier was summoned to assist at Kolberg, but left General Granjean's division at Stralsund to man the trenches. Unsurprisingly, as soon as Mortier disappeared over the horizon, Essen launched an attack on the lonesome Granjean, forcing him to retire. Soon a major Swedish offensive was under way, and by 7 April Granjean found himself almost 100 miles (160.9km) south-east of Stralsund, seeking sanctuary at Stettin. Rushing back to retrieve the situation, Mortier arrived at Stettin six days later and mounted an immediate counter-attack at the head of 12,000 troops. The marshal's advance – launched amid violent storms of hail and rain – succeeded in driving the Swedes back on Stralsund. But on 17 April Mortier proposed a ceasefire. Essen – increasingly isolated, not to say, disillusioned by lack of support – was happy to agree and on 29 April talks resulted in the Armistice of Schlachtow. The terms of the armistice suited both sides: Essen would be left in peace at Stralsund as long as he stayed-put, and Mortier would be free to join Napoleon's spring offensive against Bennigsen. Essen remained in possession of Stralsund until August, when, following the Peace of Tilsit, Gustavus ordered his evacuation.

In the southern province of Silesia, Jérôme Bonaparte had been given the task of mopping up Prussian resistance. His campaign began in December 1806 with the investment of Breslau, almost 200 miles (321.8km) south-west of Warsaw, on the banks of the Oder. The city was a major fortress, surrounded by steep walls and deep moats. Initially, Jérôme's 22,000 Bavarians and Württembergers had little to do but destroy suburbs and bridges. Once the Nikolai and Ohlau suburbs were razed, however, Jérôme's guns could reach the fortress, which cradled the Old Town. A heavy bombardment followed, sending Breslau's citizens scurrying underground for safety. Apparently, some were deafened by the ferocity of the cannonade, which claimed 160 innocent lives and as many ancient buildings. Negotiations for the city's surrender started when a Prussian relief force failed to break through and the place fell into Jérôme's hands on 7 January 1807. But Bonaparte was not satisfied with possessing the fortress, preferring to tear down its walls: replacing them with boulevards and plazas. Young, inexperienced, arrogant, Napoleon's youngest brother was never going to win a 'hearts and minds' campaign in Silesia, as Karl Wilhelm Ferdinand von Funck, adjutant-general to the king of Saxony, observes:

'His rapid rise in rank had fostered all the self-confidence of one born in the purple with the hotheadedness of an undisciplined, wealthy youngster. Because he had grown up to be the brother of the most powerful monarch in the world, he regarded nothing as impossible; everything had, in his opinion, to give way to his mere wishes, his whims, and even every naughtiness whereby he meant no harm had to be permitted him. He was therefore capable of committing acts of great harshness and injustice, not of any evil intent, but from sheer irresponsibility. Human beings did not count at all in his eyes. They were only there to submit to every whim of the Bonaparte family, called by destiny to rule over them.'

A man of little military expertise, Jérôme relieved heavily on his experienced lieutenant, General Vandamme. But this officer – though undoubtedly capable – was a noted brigand, constantly on the look-out for loot. Napoleon, meanwhile, milked Silesia for all it was worth, to finance the war effort. Thus, Silesia suffered as Jérôme's IX Corps continued its south-westward slog down the banks of the Oder.

On 10 January Schweidnitz was invested by Vandamme with 8,000 Württembergers. The fortress was held by 6,000 Prussians, but during the course of the siege some 1,000 deserted. According to Petre, Schweidnitz capitulated on 11 April, its surviving Prussians marching into captivity.

On 12 January, Bavarian troops under General von Deroy arrived before Brieg on the west bank of the Oder. Five days later the fortress fell, the 1,500-strong Prussian garrison having sustained less than twenty casualties. Napoleon announced the capture of Brieg in his 53rd Bulletin, claiming his troops were warm, well-fed and in good health. But the reverse was true, with soldiers marching on empty stomachs through bitter weather.

By 24 January, General von Deroy's Bavarians had reached Kosel, another bastion on the Oder. But the campaign was beginning to tell on IX Corps, its strength drained by battle, sickness, and the need to garrison its conquests. Manpower was also reduced by Napoleon's constant demand for reinforcements. Consequently, 6,000 Bavarians besieged 4,500 Prussians at Kosel with little effect. The affair dragged on till 2 July, when news of Napoleon's victory at Friedland persuaded the Bavarians to pack their bags.

By now – having taken Neisse, Glatz and Silberberg in June – IX Corps was reduced to 2,629 Bavarians and 5,640 Württembergers: a total of just 8,269. For Jérôme and Vandamme, victory had come just in time.

unleashing the beast of inflation. Meanwhile, despite Napoleon's insistence the city is to recover its status as a 'free' port, Danzig is occupied by French troops, governed by a French general, and forced to join the emperor's Continental System. Trade war with Britain leads to a strict blockade by the Royal Navy, effectively cutting off seaborne trade – the city's very lifeblood.

Thus ends one of the few great sieges of the Napoleonic Wars to take place outside the Spanish peninsula. But if Kalkreuth is to be believed, the crowning cause of the city's fall is Polish patriotism: manifesting itself as fraternization with, and desertion to, the besieging legions. Be that as it may, the 'liberation' of Danzig ushers in seven years of poverty and hardship, ending with Napoleon's fall and a return to Prussian rule – despite public protests – in 1814. Danzig will not be Polish until 1945.

2–7 June 1807: Bennigsen's Spring Offensive

By the time Danzig falls on 27 May 1807 Napoleon has over 200,000 troops in Poland. These include the veterans of his Grand Army, augmented by conscripts from France (called up a year before their time), drafts from allied nations, and Polish volunteers. Clearly, Napoleon is stacking the cards in his favour, but the ultimate goal of defeating the Russian Army and bringing Alexander to the bargaining table is yet to be realized. But with Danzig taken and the campaigning season close, Napoleon is confident enough to plan a final effort, setting a date of 10 June for the projected onslaught. But Bennigsen has other ideas.

By the end of May 1807 Bennigsen has concentrated over 50,000 troops at Heilsberg, on the River Alle. He has advanced to within striking distance of the Grand Army as part of a plan, concocted by Alexander and Frederick William, calling for a frontal assault across the Passarge, aided by Allied break-outs along the Baltic. But the plan – which envisaged the deployment of British, Prussian, Russian, Swedish and perhaps even Austrian forces – has been scuppered by the fall of Danzig. But instead of calling off the Passarge offensive and opening up peace talks, Alexander and Frederick William have left Bennigsen to go it alone.

On 2 June 1807 the bulk of the Grand Army is strung out along the River Passarge, its left-wing resting on the Baltic, its right on Warsaw. As previously mentioned, I Corps holds the extreme left, or northern, flank and V Corps – now under Masséna – the extreme right, with IV, VI and III Corps in-between. Each corps is roughly a day's march from its neighbour. Bernadotte's I Corps has established a bridgehead on the right bank of the Passarge at Spanden, Soult's IV Corps one upstream at Lomitten. Ney's VI Corps sits 10 miles (16km) in advance of the Passarge at Guttstadt, on the Alle. Davout's III Corps is situated at Osterode, over 20 miles (32km) south-west of Guttstadt (Napoleon and the Imperial Guard are almost 50 miles (80.4km) behind the front line at Finkenstein). The arrangement of the corps described above resembles a huge

Napoleon at Finkenstein

After Eylau, as we have seen, Napoleon withdrew to Osterode, leaving the Russians free to reclaim the town and its grim battlefield in the days to come. But on 1 April 1807 the emperor quit Osterode for Finkenstein, some 30 miles (48.2km) to the north-east. With the front line seemingly quiet, interest shifted to Danzig, and Napoleon – expecting a Russian expedition to relieve the threatened city – wanted to be nearer the action.

Finkenstein was a country estate belonging to a court chamberlain of the king of Prussia. A picturesque place some 50 miles (80.4km) south-east of Danzig, Napoleon took up residence with his headquarters staff, the Imperial Guard, and mistress, Marie Walewska in tow. According to the Saxon diplomat, von Funck:

'Finkenstein is a mansion pure and simple without a village, only a cluster of small, one-storied houses for the occupation of its employees, now overcrowded by the staff of the imperial court. The guard, which was relieved every day and drawn from the neighbouring cantonments, was only 100 strong, even the prince of Neufchâtel's [i.e. Berthier] general staff was crowded out of Finkenstein and billeted with General Camus in the little town of Rosenberg some 10 miles away. The cantonments were distributed in such a way that it was possible to reach Finkenstein without encountering one of them. The castle grounds had no other enclosure than a sunk fence, which I often crossed without being challenged by the few sentries posted along it. An extensive wood, several miles long, in which it was easy to approach under cover, extended to within 150 paces of this ditch. Napoleon's rooms in the first storey gave on to the gardens, the guardroom was on the opposite side in the courtyard, and he himself was in the habit of strolling about the gardens with only Berthier or one or two generals in attendance. The Prussians could hardly have failed to have an accurate map of the country and information of the conditions which every inhabitant of the countryside knew. Nothing would have been easier than a raid on headquarters, but at that time they did not know how to use the Cossacks.'

It was at Finkenstein that Napoleon concluded a treaty with envoys from the Shah of Persia. The Shah – who had territorial ambitions in Georgia and Transcaucasia – had been at war with Russia since December 1806. Napoleon wanted to exploit the situation by making a public gesture of support for the Shah: thus forcing Alexander to divert troops bound for Poland to his shore up Persian border. The Franco–Persian accord – the so-called Treaty of Finkenstein, signed on 4 May 1807 – stipulated French protection for Persia, support for her territorial claims, and military aid for her army. In return, the Shah was required to break off ties with Britain and join a projected invasion of British India. But despite the pledges and public displays of friendship, the Treaty of Finkenstein came to nothing: Napoleon's imminent triumphs at Friedland and Tilsit making it redundant. Thus, the terms of the treaty were never realized, and by 1809 the Shah was batting for England.

2–7 June 1807: Bennigsen's Spring Offensive

Area of operations between 4–12 June 1807 – a detail from Petre's map of 1901.

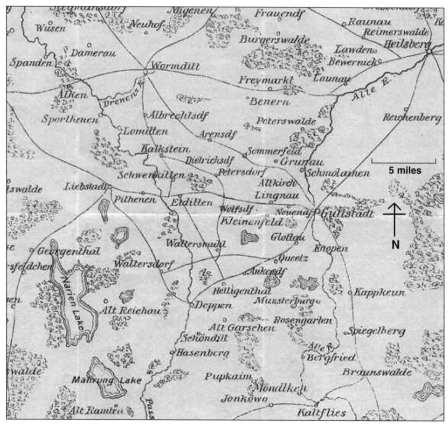

Detail from Petre's 1901 map showing the area to the west of Guttstadt and Heilsberg.

arrowhead, with VI Corps as the point. But Ney's position is a vulnerable one. If attacked, the marshal will have to scramble across the Passarge, a day's march in his rear, to escape being cut off: a fact not lost on Bennigsen, who has selected VI Corps as the prime target for a surprise attack.

Bennigsen's plan is to launch diversionary attacks on Bernadotte at Spanden and Soult at Lomitten, while concentrating his main effort against Ney at Guttstadt. The offensive is announced for 4 June, with Lestocq's Prussians tackling Bernadotte, and Doctorov's 7th Division hitting Soult. Bennigsen himself will attack Ney, with a view to surrounding VI Corps, cutting it off, and annihilating it. According to Petre: 'The scheme had in its favour the fact that Ney, his front being surrounded by forests, could not see what was going on at any considerable distance.' But apart from carving up Ney, it is unclear what Bennigsen hopes to achieve. As far as the 'big picture' is concerned, Napoleon now holds the upper hand: any laurels likely to come Bennigsen's way can only be localized, limited to the 'little picture', and dependent upon the use of surprise tactics.

2–7 June 1807: Bennigsen's Spring Offensive

And yet Bennigsen manages to compromise even this window of opportunity. At the last minute, he postpones his offensive for twenty-four hours: but word fails to reach General von Rembow, whose 6,000 Prussians begin their attack at Spanden on the 4th as previously agreed. With Prussian guns blazing away at French positions along the Passarge, a courier from Doctorov arrives demanding to know what von Rembow is about. Updated on Bennigsen's revised schedule, von Rembow – confused, embarrassed, furious, or a combination of all three – calls off the assault. But the damage is done: Bernadotte being forewarned of imminent danger. Thus, Bennigsen loses the initiative before his battles have begun.

At 10.00 a.m. next day, the Prussians return to the attack: the French are waiting for them. Meanwhile, under Lestocq's influence, von Rembow has decided to escalate the operation at Spanden from a sideshow into a major event. Thus, after a bombardment lasting two hours, the Prussians – aided by two Russian infantry regiments – advance on General Frère's prepared positions in an all-out attack. Petre describes the sequel:

> 'Waiting till the enemy were at point-blank range, the 27th received them with such a murderous fire that they were driven off with heavy loss and pursued by the 17th Dragoons issuing from the bridge, towards Wusen. In this fight Bernadotte, wounded in the head by a musket ball, had to make over command of the corps to Dupont, who, next day, handed it over to Victor.'

So ends the attack on Spanden: a débâcle costing Bennigsen at least 500 casualties, not to mention the element of surprise – the crucial element of his original plan. The affair highlights poor staff work, resulting in a lamentable breakdown in communications between Bennigsen, Lestocq and von Rembow.

On the same day, 5 June, Doctorov attacks Soult at Lomitten, in accordance with Bennigsen's new timetable. The Russian assault begins at 8.00 a.m. with 7th Division's emergence from the Forest of Albrechtsdorf. Doctorov's 12,000 troops advance on the bridgehead at Lomitten in three great columns, while horsemen of the Ekaterinoslav Dragoons and Kiev Hussars splash into the river to search for a ford. The bridgehead is held by some 6,000 troops under General St Cyr, augmented by two batteries of 12-pounders, and protected by earthworks and an abatis of felled tree trunks. The ensuing battle is a bloody one: the bastion changing hands several times. According to Petre: 'Again and again the Russians attempted the storm of the bridgehead. This fierce combat had raged for eight hours when a final effort was made in a single column. Success was almost within its grasp, when a splendid charge, by two French battalions, snatched victory from it.' Nevertheless, Doctorov's artillery fire is so intense that St Cyr forsakes the right bank, and by 8.00 p.m. – with the village of Lomitten ablaze – withdraws to prepared positions on the left bank. Having forced this retreat, however, Doctorov considers his job done: for instead of carrying the bridge, he falls back on Albrechtsdorf, signalling the end of the fight.

But as Petre states: 'The actions at Spanden and Lomitten were but a cover to the more serious attempt, which was simultaneously made, to cut off Ney's corps in its exposed position about Guttstadt.' For his *pièce de résistance*, Bennigsen has assembled some 50,000 troops. Facing them are approximately 15,000 Frenchmen. The Russian attack goes in at 6.00 a.m. and confronted with such a staggering show of force, Ney has little choice but to retire on Ankendorf, several miles south-west of Guttstadt, on the Deppen road. According to Petre: 'the marshal, finding himself greatly outnumbered, fell back in first-rate order on Ankendorf, fighting every step of the way, and holding every fold of the ground with strong swarms of skirmishers; Gortchakov, meanwhile, occupied Guttstadt, which Ney had abandoned.' Despite this initial failure to crush VI Corps, Bennigsen hopes for success on the morrow, and his official dispatch for 5 June remains upbeat, blithely exaggerating Ney's losses and the extent of his retreat:

> 'General Ney's corps is defeated, and General Roget, several officers, with about 2,000 rank and file, have been taken prisoners; the enemy's loss in killed amounts to 2,000; on our side it is not very considerable. During the action which took place on the left bank of the Alle, Lieutenant General Prince Gortchakov rendered himself master of Guttstadt, and took a considerable magazine. The enemy was pursued for 4 German miles [i.e. over 18 English miles].'

Next morning sees Ney holding his ground at Ankendorf, Bennigsen's advance guard steadily approaching. Determined to destroy his wily adversary, Bennigsen issues his orders at 5.00 a.m.: Prince Gallitzin to advance on Deppen to sever Ney's escape route over the Passarge; General Baron Sacken to advance against the marshal's centre; General Gortchakov to envelop the French right; Prince Bagration and the Grand Duke Constantine to remain in reserve. But Ney deftly outmanoeuvres the ponderous Russian commanders – whose operations are severely hampered by lakes, woods and marshes – falling back in good order. He slips from Bennigsen's grasp at Deppen, disappearing over the Passarge, burning the bridge after him. It has taken the bulk of Bennigsen's 50,000 troops three hours to hustle Ney's 15,000 a mere 2½ miles (4km). By the end of two days' fighting, Ney has lost over 2,000 men, most of them taken prisoner (including General Roget). But he has held an army at bay, gaining valuable time for his fellow marshals to assemble and react. It is a notable achievement, demonstrating skilful use of terrain and general mastery of the art of retreat. Bennigsen has also

2–7 June 1807: Bennigsen's Spring Offensive

lost some 2,000 casualties, with Generals Ostermann-Tolstoi and Somov among the wounded.

Bennigsen is naturally furious at Ney's miraculous getaway: outnumbered by over three-to-one, it seems inconceivable the French marshal has not been crushed. Fuming at what he sees as a fiasco, Bennigsen turns on his divisional commanders, especially Sacken, whom he accuses of allowing Ney to escape: 'Bennigsen … seems to have expressed himself so freely,' writes Petre, 'that Sacken left the army temporarily.' But as ever, Bennigsen's official dispatches to the tsar remain positive:

> 'General Ney's corps, which on its retreat took a strong position near Arensdorf [Ankendorf?] was this day attacked at three o'clock in the morning, routed on all points, and forced to fall back to the Passarge. The enemy's loss is very considerable, and amounts merely in prisoners taken in the course of these two days to sixty field and other officers, and at least to 1,500 rank and file …'

Finally, to add insult to injury, Bennigsen falls victim to a French ploy that stops his advance in its tracks. On 7 June he receives a captured dispatch, addressed to Ney and signed by Berthier, stating that Marshal Davout is about to fall on the Russian rear with 40,000 troops. Thrown into a panic, the credulous Bennigsen immediately shifts into reverse, ordering a retreat: first on Guttstadt, and then on the entrenched camp at Heilsberg (Lestocq's Prussians will fall back on Königsberg). But the dispatch is bogus, planted on the Russians in an effort to save Ney from further molestation. And so Bennigsen, tricked by a *ruse de guerre*, is running away from shadows. Yet given the overall strategic picture, retreat is the only realistic option, as noted by historian Hilaire Belloc:

> 'Bennigsen, having failed in this attempt at a surprise stroke, had nothing to do but fall back along the main road which leads to Königsberg, for his numbers were inferior to those which the emperor could bring now against him … On the other hand he felt fairly sure … of being able to maintain the defensive indefinitely as he so fell back … first of all he had heavily fortified Heilsberg, a place on the main road two days' march from the extreme point of the French front; and next because he had proved during all the winter fighting the stubbornness of the Russian line. Round Heilsberg he had five redoubts and sixteen entrenched batteries and a three-quarter circle facing the French, making a convex front of some 4 to 5 miles round the town. To attack such strength might well exhaust enemy forces superior to his own by only a quarter, and if they should attempt to make him retire by turning those works, he would have ample time behind a good defensive to fall back after having badly mauled his opponent.'

Campaign Chronicle

7–12 June 1807: The Battle of Heilsberg

'I am very happy to see the enemy wished to avoid our coming to him,' comments Napoleon on hearing of Bennigsen's attacks along the Passarge. He quits Finkenstein for the front on 5 June, riding in an open carriage surrounded by bodyguards, later switching to horseback. The emperor, with the whole Grand Army in his wake, is riding towards the final showdown with Bennigsen. It is time to make the Polish gamble pay off.

Napoleon approaches Deppen on 7 June. Stretching miles to the rear, his columns advance: toiling up dusty dirt tracks in suffocating heat. Each man is carrying extra cartridges, and supply waggons sag under the weight of artillery ammunition. Since Mohrungen, 15 miles (24km) west of Deppen, the troops have breathed the scent of war: burning houses, rotting corpses. Napoleon finds Deppen a ruin, torched by Bennigsen before turning-tail for Guttstadt. According to Pierre François Percy, Napoleon's Organizer of Military Heath Services: 'We stopped for a meal; a beautiful young girl stared hungrily at my hunk of black bread ... I offered her a crust; she blushed and put it into her mouth. Eating with difficulty, she turned away and wept. I had given her a glass of brandy, which she swallowed from politeness.'

Napoleon is delighted by developments, but remains puzzled about Bennigsen's motives: 'Everything leads to the belief that the enemy is on the move, though it is ridiculous on his part to engage in a general action now that Danzig is taken ... The whole thing smells of a rash move.' Unsure of his enemy's whereabouts, Napoleon orders Murat forward to find prisoners. On the following day, 8 June, the emperor is presented with captives from Bagration's rearguard. They tell of Bennigsen's march on Guttstadt. Napoleon orders an immediate advance, led by Murat's 12,000 troopers. Among their number is Sous-Lieutenant de Gonneville of the 6th Cuirassiers: 'We found the villages fearfully devastated, the inhabitants fled or dead in their homes; in one of them there were five corpses side by side, and a child of twelve still breathing. Colonel d'Avenay took him, had him attended to, saved his life, and then kept him as a servant, and left him a sum of sixty pounds by will ...'

Murat drives Bagration back on Guttstadt, where, aided by Platov's Cossacks, the Russian general makes a gallant stand. Bagration holds out until the arrival of Ney's infantry around 8.00 p.m. Then he slips over the Alle, and melting into the dusk, follows the rest of Bennigsen's force to Heilsberg.

Napoleon enters Guttstadt on 9 June but does not tarry long. The pursuit is to continue, and Murat's advance guard will lock horns with Bagration's rearguard once more. Meanwhile, peasants are recruited to dig defensive ditches and prepare earthworks (in case of a Russian counter-attack), while starving Frenchmen strip their fields bare.

7–12 June 1807: The Battle of Heilsberg

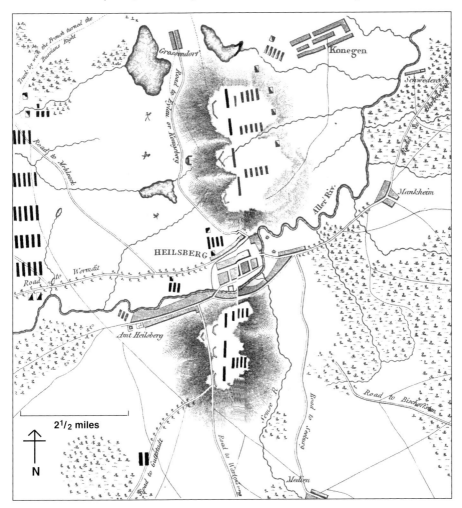

The Battle of Heilsberg, 10 June 1807. This is Wilson's battle map of 1810, clearly indicating the formidable line of Russian redoubts on high ground flanking the town.

At dawn on 10 June the bulk of the Grand Army quits Guttstadt, striking north-east up the parched road to Heilsberg, some 12 miles (19.3km) beyond. Meanwhile, Murat makes good progress, reaching the outskirts of town before 10.00 a.m. Following him, at some distance, are the corps of Soult and Lannes (leading the 'Reserve Army' from Danzig). According to F.D. Logan:

> 'Heilsberg lies in a hollow on the left bank of the Alle, which is crossed here
> by three bridges. The rising ground, which surrounded the town, had been
> fortified by the Russians during the spring by a line of redoubts on either
> bank. The south side of the river was thickly wooded. On the north side,

Prince Bagration (1765–1812). Adored by the Russian soldiers, the reckless Georgian prince distinguished himself as Bennigsen's advance guard commander.

west of Heilsberg, there was a slightly undulating plain across which, and parallel to, the Russian position, flowed the Spuibach. To facilitate communication with either bank Bennigsen had constructed several bridges. The Russian Army was drawn up on both sides of the river, four divisions and most of the cavalry being on the left, and five divisions on the right bank.'

Bennigsen's position at Heilsberg is unassailable: at least by means of a frontal attack. The Russians hold the advantages of high ground, prepared defences, and superiority of numbers. They cannot be evicted from of Heilsberg at the sword's point, but must be manoeuvred out by an outflanking operation. But the need for such a finesse is lost on the hothead Murat, who leads his unsupported cavalry to the attack.

As advance guard commander, Murat's job is to probe Bennigsen's strength and reconnoitre the ground before Napoleon's arrival. But having driven the Russians from the outlying village of Launau, he boldly advances to Bevernick, a stone's throw from Bennigsen's batteries, overlooking Heilsberg's western approaches. Here his attack stalls, brought to a halt by Russian artillery fire. Frustrated, and already in a filthy temper, Murat must wait for Soult's infantry before pressing on.

7–12 June 1807: The Battle of Heilsberg

About 3.30 p.m. General Savary arrives before Bevernick with two infantry regiments and six guns. The village is quickly carried, but Murat's troopers are scattered by Russian cavalry and the French are halted once more. Meanwhile, the remainder of Soult's infantry battles forward to Heilsberg, raked by volleys from guns on the opposite bank of the Alle. Progress is painfully slow and Murat – kitted out in a flashy white uniform and red Moroccan leather boots – is reduced to the role of spectator. Having already accused Savary of cowardice – prompting the observation that Murat wanted 'less courage and more common sense' – Napoleon's cavalry supremo decides to take matters into his own hands. With no possible target but Bennigsen's now passive squadrons, Murat orders a charge, as witnessed by de Gonneville of the 6th Cuirassiers, part of General d'Espagne's command:

> 'At this moment the grand duke of Berg (Murat) came up to us; he came from our right rear, followed by his staff, passed at a gallop across our front, bending forwards on his horse's neck, and as he passed at full speed by General Espagne, he flung at him one word alone which I heard, "Charge!" This order, given without any further directions for an attack on sixty squadrons of picked men, by fifteen unsupported squadrons, seemed to me the more difficult to understand, since in order to get at the enemy there was a nearly impracticable ravine to be crossed by twos and fours, and it was then necessary to form under the enemy's fire 100 paces from his first line. In case of a check we had no possible means of retreat, but the order was given and the thing had to be done …'

And done it is. Altogether, de Gonneville's regiment charges six times, and by day's end, each man's sabre will be dripping with blood. As for Murat, he throws himself into the thick of the fighting, heedless of all danger, as his biographer, Atteridge, describes:

> 'The cavalry was engaged with a superior force of eighty Russian squadrons, and there was hard hand-to-hand fighting. Murat had a narrow escape. Charging beside Lasalle, at the head of the hussars and *chasseurs*, he had his horse killed under him. He caught and mounted a riderless horse, but was hardly in the saddle again when he was cut off and surrounded by a party of Russian dragoons. He was fighting for his life, when Lasalle in person arrived to the rescue, cutting down several of the enemy. A few minutes later, Murat saved Lasalle's life in the mêlée: "We are quits now, my dear general," he said, grasping his hand.'

But the bloodshed continues and Murat has a second horse killed under him. A corporal of cuirassiers offers the marshal his mount, and off Murat

Campaign Chronicle

The Battle of Heilsberg, 10 June 1807 (contemporary print). The futile battle for Bennigsen's entrenched camp cost almost 20,000 casualties in all. In the end, Napoleon simply manoeuvred the Russians out of Heilsberg.

gallops, leaving a red Moroccan boot in one of the stirrups of the dead horse.

Napoleon arrives too late to stop Murat's madness, but even with the emperor present, the folly continues, as Marshal Lannes – appearing around 10.00 p.m. – launches a fruitless assault on Bennigsen's redoubts under cover of darkness. This act of lunacy – doubtless intended to impress the emperor – results in 3,000 needless casualties to add to the 10,000 already suffered. By 11.00 p.m. the fighting finally fades, both sides leaving the battlefield to the locals, who, like a legion of ghouls, come to strip the dead. Meanwhile, Sous-Lieutenant de Gonneville returns to his bivouac, famished, fatigued, and bloodstained:

'The baggage had not come up; we had no bread or anything else to eat. I had a little tea made in a bit of a canister shot case. The ground was covered pieces of these cases, and shot and muskets. The day was spent in

7–12 June 1807: The Battle of Heilsberg

burying our dead, and putting the living in order as far as might be …
Next day, about five in the morning, the train arrived. We had bread, but
very little of it; General Renauld gave me half a bottle of beer, which I
shared with Marulaz; since the preceding evening we had been living on
the grass, which we plucked and chewed … the emperor passed through
us, and was saluted by acclamations to which he seemed to pay no
attention, appearing gloomy and out of spirits. We learnt later that he had
no intention of attacking the Russians so seriously as had been done, and
especially had desired not to engage his cavalry. The grand duke of Berg
had been reprimanded for this, and followed the emperor with a tolerably
sheepish air. We again passed the night on the field of battle, lying side by
side with the dead; then next day we commenced our march, after getting
a ration of bread.'

Another hungry soldier is Jean-Baptiste Barrès, who beds down on the battlefield
with his comrades of the Imperial Guard: 'The day closed without result, each
side retaining its positions, and we bivouacked on the ground we occupied,
amidst the dead of the morning's battle. We had been twelve hours under arms,
without changing our position.'

But there is no rest for Bennigsen. Sick with fever (he fell unconscious from
his horse several times during the battle), midnight finds him scribbling his
report to the tsar:

'This day at noon Bonaparte attacked the Russian Army in the position on
the left bank of the Alle with his whole force. A short time before the
attack, Prince Bagration was detached to Launau, where he was attacked by
a force greatly superior; and was obliged to fall back. A considerable
number of troops then received orders to advance from every quarter,
while others formed the reserve. The firing began on all points, and the
enemy was forced to leave the field of battle to the Russian troops, who
acquired new glory on that day. The loss cannot yet be ascertained, but it is
very considerable on both sides; and amounts on the part of the French, at
least to 12,000 men in killed and wounded …'

At dawn on 11 June the men of both sides meet in silence to remove their
wounded and bury their dead. Another costly battle of attrition is expected by
all, but suddenly – too late for over 20,000 maimed or murdered men – the rival
commanders come to their senses: Heilsberg can only be taken by a turning
action. And so, as Napoleon prepares to march around the town's flanks,
Bennigsen prepares to evacuate. Russian guns still boom throughout the day, but
as soon as night falls, Bennigsen quits:

'finding that the enemy might cut off all provisions from my army in its present position, and detach a corps to Königsberg, I humbly beg leave to state to your royal Majesty, my determination to quit this place tonight, and march to another position near Schippenbeil, in order to be able to protect those behind the Alle, the transport of provisions etc., and in case the enemy marches to Königsberg, to follow him immediately.'

And at 4.00 a.m. on 12 June, the French hit town. On entering Heilsberg, they find piles of provisions, stores and wounded: all abandoned by Bennigsen in his haste to escape encirclement. But Heilsberg cannot be described as a French success. As at Eylau, Napoleon is left in possession of a battlefield, not a decisive victory. As F.D. Logan states: 'Heilsberg is only one more instance of the failure of a frontal attack carried out by successive assaults and with no attempt at combined action by the different corps. The position was strong and the assailants were inferior in numbers ...'

12–15 June 1807: Königsberg and the Battle of Friedland

Having quit Heilsberg in the early hours of 12 June, Bennigsen reaches the safety of the Alle's right bank. Despite the hasty withdrawal, he is claiming Heilsberg as a victory. His troops, however, are bewildered, even disgusted, at the evacuation of a seemingly impregnable position – not to mention the abandonment of a battle they were apparently winning. But Bennigsen is fretting about being outflanked, surrounded, cut off from the long road home.

Bennigsen is also concerned about Königsberg, his last remaining depot. He has little doubt Napoleon will march on the city, and if his last missive to Alexander is to be believed, intends contesting possession of the place ('and in case the enemy marches to Königsberg, to follow him immediately ...'). Some sources claim Bennigsen now orders his Prussian ally, Lestocq – hopelessly cut off by French forces and stranded some 30 miles north-west of Heilsberg on the shores of the Frische Haff – to fall back on Königsberg with all speed, in order to reach it ahead of the French. Other sources say Lestocq makes this manoeuvre on his own initiative; and still others that the Prussian general was simply shepherded towards Königsberg by encircling enemies. Whatever the truth of these assertions, the immediate aftermath of Heilsberg sees Lestocq retreating north-east to Königsberg, and Bennigsen retreating north up the right bank of the Alle, apparently making for the same goal.

But Bennigsen appears to have been torn between the need to cover Königsberg and the desire to keep his own army in tact. Although most sources echo Bennigsen's declaration that he is Königsberg-bound, evidence suggests he is fact making for Wehlau, some 50 miles (80.4km) north of Heilsberg and 30 miles (48.2km) east of Königsberg. From Wehlau (where the

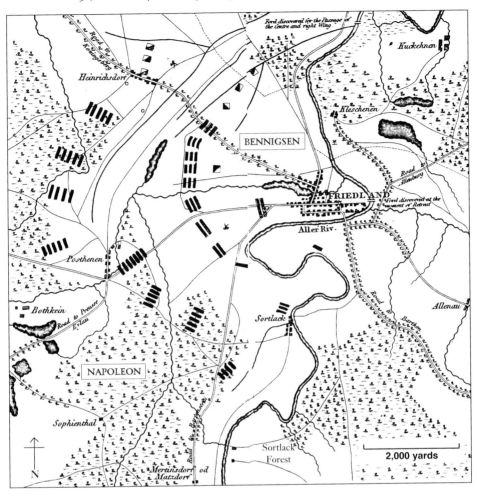

The Battle of Friedland, 14 June 1807 – Wilson's battle map of 1810.

Alle flows into the Pregel) Bennigsen might march west to Königsberg: but as the city would probably have fallen into French hands in the meantime, such a course of action seems illogical. More likely, Bennigsen plans to continue north-east to the River Niemen and the safety of the Russian border. But whatever Bennigsen's ultimate purpose – something debated by historians ever since – Fate will take the general's hand and lead him west across the Alle at Friedland …

Napoleon is also concerned about Königsberg. For him it is the key to victory. Not only does he need the city's stores to victual his army (which, despite stripping the land bare cannot subsist in this fashion indefinitely), he also needs a decisive showdown with Bennigsen, to bring the campaign to a successful

125

Campaign Chronicle

The Battle of Friedland, 14 June 1807 (contemporary print). In this version, Russian grenadiers fire a volley at the approaching French, while comrades plunge into the Alle to escape the onslaught.

conclusion. And as Napoleon believes Bennigsen must fall back on his base or lose the war, a drive on Königsberg would seem to kill two birds with one stone: gaining supplies for his soldiers, while forcing Bennigsen to make a stand.

With this strategy in mind, the emperor's only concern is: where will Bennigsen recross the Alle? Between Heilsberg and Königsberg there are several crossing points, the most likely being Friedland, with a usable road linking it to Königsberg in the north-west. The emperor detaches Marshal Lannes to reconnoitre the area. Meanwhile, the rest of the army is split in two: Murat, at the head of perhaps 60,000 men (9,000 cavalry plus Soult's IV Corps, with Davout's III Corps in support) will march directly on Königsberg – capturing the city if possible – while Napoleon will lead his remaining 80,000 troops to Eylau – a day's march west of Friedland – to await developments.

On 13 June, Napoleon's scouts report that Bennigsen is continuing his hike north up the right bank of the Alle. The emperor urges Lannes to occupy Domnau and push patrols towards nearby Friedland. Some sources claim Lannes

12–15 June 1807: Königsberg and the Battle of Friedland

General (later Marshal) Victor (1764–1841). Sent in January 1807 to take command of the newly-formed X Corps, Victor was captured by Prussian troops disguised as peasants. Indignant, he wrote a letter to Napoleon, asking him to lodge an official complaint with the king of Prussia! Victor was released on 8 March 1807, in exchange for Blücher, of Waterloo fame. He fought at Friedland, replacing the wounded Bernadotte at the head of I Corps, and was made a marshal shortly after.

is to seize the bridges in rear of the town. At any rate, by midday four squadrons of French hussars – the van of Lannes' advance guard – reach Friedland, making themselves at home.

But at 3.00 p.m. Bennigsen's advance guard – consisting of 3,000 cavalrymen under Prince Gallitzin – arrives opposite the picturesque riverside town. Hearing of the weak French presence, the Russians cross the Alle and evict Lannes' troopers, as described by Louis Lejeune: 'On 13 June the Russians, in retreat on the right bank of the Alle, noticed that our light cavalry, in endeavouring to bar their way to Königsberg, where their magazines were situated, had taken possession of Friedland, and Prince Bagration ordered a large body of cavalry to charge our advance guard, routing them and compelling them to retire behind the advancing infantry of General Oudinot.'

But not all the hussars make good their escape, Gallitzin bagging prisoners who tell of Lannes' imminent arrival from the west. According to their testimony, Lannes' force is weak, isolated, its advance guard consisting of a single division. When Bennigsen arrives a few hours later, he is presented with the captives, and according to Wilson: 'From the information of the prisoners, General Bennigsen believed that Oudinot's corps, so shattered at Heilsberg, was alone stationed at Posthenen, about 3 miles in front of Friedland, on the road to Königsberg. Having occupied the town, and thrown forward some cavalry to cover it from insult during the night, he determined, at 4 o'clock in the morning, to fall upon Oudinot with a division and complete his extinction …'

And so, whatever Bennigsen's original intention, he now commits himself to a passage of the Alle at Friedland. He apparently does so on the strength of information proffered by a handful of French prisoners, and without knowing Napoleon's precise whereabouts. Bennigsen apparently calculates he will have time to cross the Alle in force, defeat Oudinot – even Lannes if necessary – and disappear back across the river before Napoleon can interfere. This plan seems to indicate that Bennigsen was heading for Wehlau after all.

Meanwhile, Lannes is assembling his force on the plain west of Friedland, having slogged up the Eylau road via Domnau. His 'Reserve Army', consisting of the divisions of Generals Oudinot and Verdier, numbers no more than 15,000, having suffered badly in the night attack on Heilsberg. Finding the town in enemy hands – but unsure of the numbers facing him – Lannes sends word to Napoleon at Eylau. The emperor receives this message around 9.00 p.m. but does not know what to make of it: is Lannes faced with the whole Russian Army or merely an advance guard? Napoleon sends Mortier's VIII Corps to Lannes' aid, plus Grouchy's dragoon division. Later – following the arrival of more detailed reports – he will despatch Ney and Nansouty's cuirassiers. But these troops will not reach Friedland for some hours, and the emperor will not quit Eylau till the following morning. For the time being, Lannes is on his own …

Back at Friedland, Bennigsen orders pontoon bridges to be thrown across the Alle, to speed up his deployment on the left bank. As Hilaire Belloc relates, Bennigsen 'felt inclined … to break one of the fundamental rules of war because the opportunity was irresistible. Here he was, with all his forces, and nothing but Lannes' fragment in front of him: he would eat it up …'

12–15 June 1807: Königsberg and the Battle of Friedland

Having covered some 20 miles (32.1km) of his retreat on Königsberg, Lestocq's rearguard is bloodied by Soult on the evening of 13 June, in the vicinity of Kreuzburg. Falling back a further 10 miles (16km) to Gollau, Lestocq makes contact with several thousand Russian troops under Kamenski – survivors of the failed mission to Danzig. This Prusso–Russian force numbers perhaps 25,000 and succeeds in staving off further French attacks, making good its escape to Königsberg.

According to Wilson: 'When General Lestocq occupied Königsberg, he posted infantry and artillery from the Brandenburg gate to the work of Friedricksburg, and General Kamenski was charged with the defence of the Friedland gate. The enemy made several attempts to storm the Brandenburg gate, but were always repulsed with heavy loss; and to prevent cover to their future approaches, the Nassegarten suburb, and some fine mills before the Friedland gate, were set on fire and burnt.' But Petre declares it is the Allies who suffer heavy casualties, courtesy General Legrand's division from Soult's IV Corps. Either way the result is the same: the suburbs are fired and Lestocq withdraws behind the city walls, hoping against hope to be relived by Bennigsen …

Friedland is a little market town of pretty houses, pointed roofs and neat gardens. Eylau lies some 15 miles (24km) to the west, Königsberg some 30 miles (48.2) to the north-west, and Tilsit, on the Russian border, some 60 miles (96.5km) to the north-east. According to H.T. Parker, Friedland 'is built on a small peninsula of land, bounded on the south and east by the twisting Alle, on the north by the lake and marsh of the tributary Mill Stream.' The area around Friedland forms a cultivated plain, the crops standing waist-high. The peasants hereabouts are Germans: settlers devoted to tilling the soil who simply wish to be left in peace. Some $4^1/_2$ miles (7.2km) north-west of town is the village of Heinrichsdorf, straddling the Königsberg road. About 4 miles (6.4km) to the west is the village of Posthenen, on the Eylau road. And 3 miles (4.8km) to the south-west, on the steep, snaking banks of the Alle, is the village of Sortlack. It is flanked to the west by a thick forest of the same name. Friedland itself is hemmed in by water, except to the west, and as Hilaire Belloc observes: 'If one fights outside the town to the west and has to retire, one has the obstacle of the river blocking one's retreat, congesting the retiring columns in defiles. It is a maxim as old as war never to fight with one's back to a river …'

Bennigsen has a total force of over 60,000 men, and by 3.00 a.m. on 14 June 10,000 of them have crossed to the left bank of the Alle. The remainder are queuing at the bridges, patiently waiting their turn. Lannes, as we know, has no more than 15,000 troops in total. Nevertheless, the marshal has advanced to within 4 miles (6.4km) of the town, capturing the village of Posthenen in the process. But for Bennigsen, the result of the coming clash cannot be in doubt. Hilaire Belloc sets the scene: 'Bennigsen, finding in front of him at the first glimmerings of light on 14 June nothing but the advanced portion of Lannes' corps, could not resist the opportunity to turn round and eat it up.'

But as Marbot (recovered from his ordeal at Eylau and now serving on the staff of Marshal Lannes) observes: 'The difficulty which the Russians had in debouching from the town into the plain on the left bank was increased by the fact that the issue from Friedland is narrowed at that spot by a largish lake, as well as by a stream called the Mill Stream, which runs in a deep and narrow ravine.'

In fact, Friedland is a death trap, consisting of a series of defiles, almost purpose made to ensnare a large army. In order to get at his French visitors, Bennigsen has to send his troops over a kind of obstacle course: first, the Russians have to cross the Alle on narrow bridges, several of them extemporized; then they have to pass through Friedland's constricted streets; finally, they have to squeeze through a long funnel over $1^1/_2$ miles (2.75km) long and $^1/_2$ mile (0.91km) wide, created by the twisting Alle to the south and the Mill Stream (plus Mill Pond) to the north. In fact, this watercourse, extending horizontally from the Alle above Friedland as far as Posthenen, bisects the town's western approaches. Consequently, Bennigsen will have to build more bridges to give his troops access to both banks. It is bad enough for Bennigsen's infantry to negotiate these hurdles, even worse for his cavalry and artillery. Thus, although Bennigsen holds a local numerical advantage it means little, for he cannot bring it to bear – at least not swiftly enough.

Nevertheless, the passage of the Alle continues and according to Wilson, Bennigsen places his troops:

'In the open space ... between the Alle and the rivulet [Mill Stream], and about half a mile in front of Friedland ...

'General Bennigsen at first formed his troops in column, the cavalry being to the right of the Heinrichsdorf road, and as the succeeding divisions passed the Alle, the right and part of the centre of his infantry were posted between that road and the rivulet, and that part of his centre was covered by a branch of the rivulet which terminated in a broad piece of water [Mill Pond]: thus his army was entirely exposed to fire, and every movement distinctly seen; whilst the enemy were sheltered from aim, and their force and operations were concealed until they chose to expose them; moreover, upon the right of their position they had the advantage of some rising ground, which commanded both banks of the Alle as far as the town.'

Out on the plain, Lannes' line faces Friedland, stretching some 6 miles (9.9km) north to south. His left is anchored on the village Heinrichsdorf, his centre on

Posthenen, and his right on the Forest of Sortlack. All is set for what will later be dubbed the 'First Battle of Friedland'. Interestingly, the opening scene of this last battle of the campaign is an echo of the first, at Pultusk: a lonely, outnumbered Lannes facing a bold and burly Bennigsen. At 4.00 a.m. the Russian guns open up.

Bennigsen begins with an attack on Lannes' left at Heinrichsdorf. Uvarov's cavalry takes the village with infantry support, but a determined counter-attack drives both horsemen and foot soldiers out. Losses are heavy on both sides, with troops suffering horrific wounds from slashing, stabbing sabres. Lannes consolidates the success at Heinrichsdorf by detaching an infantry brigade to hold the village.

Then, on Lannes' right, a see-saw battle develops for possession of the Forest of Sortlack. Although the Russians keep clearing the woods, the French constantly reappear, the superior field craft of Lannes' light troops telling. According to Wilson, the French *voltigeurs*: 'concealed themselves from direct aim by laying down in the long grass, or behind favouring ground.' In fact, Lannes uses the high crops to his advantage: sending soldiers scuttling under cover to bob up at different points along his line, giving the impression of greater numbers.

By 8.00 a.m. Bennigsen has 40,000 troops on the left bank of the Alle, and prepares a general assault on the French line. But the arrival of Grouchy's dragoon division adds muscle to Lannes' skeleton army, raising its numbers to around 20,000. Still heavily outnumbered, the French cling on at Friedland by dint of sheer hard work, initiative, courage and tenacity. According to Lejeune:

'The united corps of grenadiers under General Oudinot, supported by General Grouchy's dragoons … had been engaged since daybreak opposite the village of Posthenen, by way of which the Russians were endeavouring to debouch with a view to a vigorous attack on us. Many charges of cavalry had taken place on the flanks of this village, whilst our infantry had been driven from it five or six times after taking possession of it. From every one of these charges our cuirassiers had brought back many prisoners, but the enemy, still supposing they had but the small body of men they could see to deal with, directed a furious cannonade upon the place …'

Lannes is reinforced further by the timely arrival of Marshal Mortier's VIII Corps, led onto the battlefield by a detachment of Dutch cavalry and Dabrowski's Poles. According to Private Daleki (quoted in Kukiel), Dabrowski urged his men on enthusiastically, despite a badly wounded leg: 'Come on, boys! Come on! The reaping is beginning! March, march Poles! Don't be, downcast – do your best!' Now Lannes has over 30,000 troops before Friedland against

Bennigsen's 45,000. Indeed, by 8.30 a.m., victory is already slipping through Bennigsen's fingers. With some 20,000 troops and most of his artillery still on the right bank, he simply cannot deploy his force fast enough to annihilate the gathering French host. In fact, Wilson claims that Bennigsen – having learned from battlefield captives that he is faced by Lannes, Grouchy and Mortier – is now so concerned about his line of retreat, he sends 6,000 troops to secure Wehlau and the road back to Russia.

And yet Lannes is still under pressure. All morning he has been sending riders to Napoleon, requesting help. The first of these, Captain Marbot (mounted on the indefatigable mare, Lisette) arrives at Eylau around 8.30 a.m., just as Napoleon is quitting the place with his remaining forces:

> 'I met the emperor leaving Eylau and found him beaming. He made me come to his side, and as we galloped I had to give him an account of all that had taken place before I left the field of battle. When I had ended my report the emperor said smiling, "Have you a good memory?" "Pretty fair, sir." "Well, what anniversary is it today, 14 June?" "Marengo." "Yes," replied the emperor, "that of Marengo; and I am going to beat the Russians as I beat the Austrians." So convinced was Napoleon on this point that as he rode along the columns, and while the soldiers saluted him with frequent cheers, he repeatedly said to them, "Today is a lucky day, the anniversary of Marengo."'

Meanwhile, the atmosphere at Friedland hots up. It is a sweltering day – over 30 degrees Celsius – and the armies of both sides are suffocating, swathed in a smog of gun smoke, tinged with the smell of cordite and blood. The Russian troops are exhausted, having marched 34 miles (54.7km) in forty-eight hours on empty stomachs. Bennigsen is demanding too much of them, and by 11.00 a.m. his attacks have run out of steam. The battle now slackens into skirmishing and sporadic cannonades.

Having succeeded in holding an army at bay, Lannes' ordeal is over. Bennigsen's is yet to begin.

By midday Napoleon is in sight of Friedland. The emperor – still accompanied by Marbot – is surrounded by his staff, his escort, and followed by the Imperial Guard plus I Corps under General Victor. Drawing nearer the battlefield, Lejeune describes how Napoleon is surprised at the scale of the action:

> 'Imagining that the Russians had only made an attack to cover the retreat of their rearguard, he was very much surprised to hear a prolonged and vigorous cannonade. In his anxiety he urged on his Arab steed, with which

few other horses could keep up, and quickly found himself among a number of wounded, who were retreating towards the ambulances. Amongst them he recognized Colonel Reynaud of the 15th Regiment of the Line, and stopped to ask him what had happened, if his regiment had retreated, and under what circumstances he had been wounded. Reynaud, who had been struck by a ball, replied that, tired of seeing his regiment inactive under a decimating fire, he had ordered it to advance and charge the enemy's guns in the hope of carrying some of them, but that a trench he had not been able to see had arrested the men, of whom he had lost 1,500 on its brink. He added: "On the plateau of Friedland, behind the position I had hoped to take, the enemy has just massed an immense number of men, certainly not less than 80,000." The emperor, still in error as to the state of things, thought this account exaggerated, and exclaimed, "That is not true!" to which Reynaud, irritated at being disbelieved, answered, "Well, I swear by my head that the numbers I have stated are there, and that there will be hot work." The emperor's only reply was to dash his spurs into his Arab, which bounded furiously forward, carrying its master into the very midst of the sharpshooters.'

Napoleon's midday arrival is apparently noted by an English officer posted in the tower of Friedland's church (though according to Wilson, the emperor is first spotted around 4.00 p.m.). The officer is Colonel John Hely Hutchinson, the ungracious, unkempt, unpopular – but intrepid – British commissioner at Bennigsen's headquarters. Bennigsen is now faced with a dilemma: he wants to withdraw from Friedland, recross the Alle, and slip away to Wehlau; but with so many defiles at his back, to attempt this in daylight would be suicide. He is effectively stuck: forced to fight it out till dark. As Petre observes: 'A general action on a favourable battlefield was what Napoleon desired above all things. At Friedland, Bennigsen gave him precisely what he wanted.'

Meanwhile, Napoleon reconnoitres the Russian position. The emperor is still unsure how many troops face him. But he can see Bennigsen is in a mess. Before him, trapped in a tight bend of the Alle, thousands of Russians are patiently standing with no hope of escape before dark. Napoleon is dumbfounded by Bennigsen's error. The situation calls for an immediate assault, but with I Corps still assembling, there is nothing to do but have lunch. Staff officers scurry to and fro, eventually finding a simple wooden chair for the emperor. Food arrives – black bread – and Napoleon sits down to eat within range of the Russian guns. Attendants beg him to withdraw, but Napoleon smiles: 'They will dine less comfortably than I shall lunch.' Meanwhile, brass hats murmur that shadows are lengthening, time is passing, and it is obviously too late to mount an attack. Napoleon silences them: 'We won't catch the enemy making a mistake like this twice.' He is right. Belloc puts it neatly: 'Bennigsen had lost his chance.'

Fortified by his frugal lunch, Napoleon calls his corps commanders together for a pre-battle conference. He describes his game plan and issues orders accordingly: there will be a powerful attack on the Russian left (Napoleon's right) at the village of Sortlack. The assault will be made by Marshal Ney's VI Corps, supported by Victor, and if necessary, the Imperial Guard. The advance is to proceed through the Forest of Sortlack, but once the enemy is engaged, Ney is to roll up the Russian left-wing: driving it round the winding river bank and funnelling it back into Friedland. Napoleon tells Ney to look neither right nor left, but to fix his sights on the church tower – temporary home of the keen-eyed Colonel Hutchinson – aiming straight for it. To support Ney's advance, the artillery will double its rate of fire, pouring shot into Bennigsen's troops caught in the killing ground between the Alle and the Mill Stream. Once inside Friedland, Ney is to seize the bridges in rear of the town, cutting off the Russian right-wing. If and when this objective is achieved, Napoleon will launch his centre (under Lannes) and his left (under Mortier) to catch the Russians between two fires. Using the Alle as his anvil, Napoleon hopes to hammer the Russians in a 'manoeuvre sur les derrières' in miniature.

With Victor's troops still panting up the Eylau road, Napoleon sets the time of Ney's assault for 5.30 p.m. and breaks up the conference. Meantime, the sun beats down and a hiatus ensues, most soldiers taking a breather. According to soldier-diplomat de Norvins, Napoleon paces up and down, lashing tall weeds with his riding crop, and chatting with Berthier: '"What's the date?" "The 14th of June, sire." "Marengo day, victory day!" returned the emperor.'

By 5.00 p.m. Victor's corps has arrived, bringing Napoleon's strength up to 80,000. All is now ready, and according to Lejeune: 'At that time the whole army was drawn up in line; Marshal Ney on the right, Marshal Lannes in the centre, Marshal Mortier on the left, and General Victor with the reserve force. The entire force of Bennigsen was in position opposite to them, in front of and on the right and left of Friedland.' As stated, Bennigsen's force is divided by the Mill Stream, which bisects his position, creating two wings. The right, under Gortchakov, lies to the north of the Mill Stream, facing Heinrichsdorf; the left, under Bagration, lies to the south, facing Posthenen, but with its extreme flank anchored on Sortlack and fronting the forest. Gallitzin's cavalry and the Russian Imperial Guard are in reserve.

But Bennigsen is beginning to consider the deployment of the two armies as academic: surely it is now too late for a general engagement? He even dares to suppose he might be permitted to slip away under cover of night after all. His hopes are dashed, however, when a movement is spotted in the French camp, and as Wilson states: 'the horizon seemed to be bound by a deep girdle of glittering steel.' But where will the blow fall? Bennigsen's *moujiks* patiently await their fate. Famished, fatigued, frying under a fierce sun, the Russians remain stoical to the last: win or lose, live or die, this is war! But Bennigsen is not so phlegmatic. He observes the French deployment with horror, regretting the detachment of 6,000 troops to Wehlau, and knowing he has wasted most of his artillery rounds on the fruitless contest with Lannes. Unable to retreat, there is nothing Bennigsen can do but accept battle.

Having reconnoitred the ground, formed his plan, marshalled his troops, and issued his orders, it is time for Napoleon to set events in motion. Now it is up to his corps commanders, their subordinates, and ultimately, the soldiers themselves. 'About half past five Marshal Ney began to move forward,' records the emperor's 79th Bulletin, 'Some shots from a battery of twenty cannon were the signal. At the same moment the division of General Marchand advanced sword in hand upon the enemy, and proceeded towards the tower of the town, being supported on the left by the division of General Bisson.'

And so Ney's advance begins, led by General Marchand's division on the right, with Bisson's division set back a little, in echelon, on the left. Latour-Maubourg's dragoon division is in support. According to one veteran, little is said, but from one end of the column to the other, one hears 'Blessed name of God, forward! Forward, sacred name of God!' Meanwhile, in the words of Baron Boulart of the Guard artillery: 'a massive bombardment announced the opening of the battle. The army was formed up and everyone was at their post. Soon musketry began to blend with the deeper groan of artillery. Incredible efforts were made on both sides, which meant it was a terrible butchery ...'

By 6.00 p.m. Ney's attack is in full swing. Having cleared the village of Sortlack, VI Corps is working its way round the twisting river bank, shunting the Russian left-wing into the narrow enclosure between the Alle and the Mill Stream. Bennigsen must react, but what to do? He orders Gortchakov to attack on the right, supported by Uvarov's cavalry, no doubt hoping to relieve pressure on his left. Meanwhile, Gallitzin's cavalry is fed across the Mill Stream, north to south, to help Bagration stem the French tide. Lejeune describes the sequel: 'Immediately a swarm of some five to six thousand Cossacks, Kalmucks and Khirgesses and Bashkirs, covering a mass of regular cavalry, surrounded our infantry, hoping to dismay them with their wild charges and yells. But our dragoons advanced at a gallop, swept aside and drove back this irregular cavalry.' According to Napoleon's 79th Bulletin, it is Latour-Maubourg's division that rescues Ney: 'When the enemy perceived that Marshal Ney had left the wood in which his right wing had been posted, they endeavoured to surround him with some regiments of cavalry, and a multitude of Cossacks, but General Latour-Maubourg's division of dragoons rode up in full gallop to the right wing, and repelled the attack of the enemy.'

Campaign Chronicle

With Gallitzin repulsed and Gortchakov making little headway against Lannes and Mortier, Bennigsen watches as Ney rounds the final bend of the river that will lead him to the gates of Friedland. At this point, Bagration's guns – aided by batteries on the right bank of the Alle – concentrate their fire on the heads of Ney's columns. Caught in a withering fire, the French attack falters then recoils. Bisson's division is caught by cavalry trying to deploy and devolves into a rabble. But Latour-Maubourg's dragoons make another desperate charge, scattering the hovering Russian horsemen, buying time for Ney's shaken infantry to rally and reform. Meanwhile, Ney's gunners put in counter-battery fire, silencing the Russian artillery, permitting the advance to continue. Finally, General Dupont's division is detached from I Corps and sent to Ney's aid.

Dupont is supported by two fifteen-gun batteries under General Sénarmont. Working their way up the Eylau road from Posthenen to the approaches of Friedland, Sénarmont's gunners eventually concentrate their cannon into a single monstrous battery. According to Napoleon's 79th Bulletin: 'General Sénarmont, who commanded the battery, pushed his works forward more than 400 paces, and greatly annoyed the enemy …' Advancing by stages, Sénarmont engages the Russians at ever shorter intervals. Soon, his gunners are slamming case shot into Bennigsen's masses at a distance of 150 yards (137m). This is eventually reduced to sixty paces. For almost half an hour the Russians absorb tremendous punishment, but as Boulart states: 'General Sénarmont blasted a hole in their line with thirty guns. They couldn't hold and were thrown back through the town …'

… To be followed by Ney and Dupont. Now Bennigsen has only one card left to play: the infantry of the Russian Imperial Guard. According to one French veteran, every Russian grenadier is a 'colossus of the North'. Charging forward with fixed bayonets, this legion of Goliaths crashes into the leading French column, and as Wilson relates: 'exacted bloody revenge, and for a moment the corps of Marshal Ney retrograded in disorder; but a reserve division advanced, obliged the guards to fall back, pressed them on, and after a further obstinate contest in the streets, forced the town.'

Louis Lejeune describes the clash from the French viewpoint:

'Marshal Ney, having quickly destroyed the forces which had opposed him, now approached Friedland by his left and attempted to enter it. The Russian Guard, infantry and cavalry together, rushed to oppose his movement, and for a moment threw the marshal's troops into confusion, making them lose ground. But Marshal Dupont [sic] saw what was going on, attacked the Russian Guard in the rear, and drove it back. With scarcely room to move in the narrow ravines by which they endeavoured to retreat, nearly all the men of the Guard fell in a general massacre, and their Generals Pahlen and Markov were killed.'

12–15 June 1807: Königsberg and the Battle of Friedland

In fact, Dupont's troops not only see off the tsar's Imperial Guard, they also repulse a further attack by Russian cavalry. Soon they are swarming onto the northern bank of the Mill Stream (thanks to Bennigsen's forsaken makeshift bridges) and into Friedland via the Königsberg road. The place is already ablaze, smitten by shells lobbed in by French howitzers. Sénarmont's battery has worked up close to the town, thundering shot into streets stuffed with retreating Russians. By 7.00 p.m. Ney is in Friedland, urging his troops forward to the bridges, past blazing buildings, through walls of Russian bayonets. Marbot describes the confusion in the streets:

> 'Ney continued his bold march, rolled back the Russians in Friedland, and entered pell-mell with them into the streets of the unlucky town, which the shells had already set on fire. There was a terrible bayonet fight, and the Russians, crowded one upon another and hardly able to move, lost very heavily. Ultimately they were obliged, in spite of their courage, to retire in disorder, and seek a refuge on the opposite bank, crossing the bridges again.'

Needless to say, Bennigsen is pulling out troops as fast as he can, making for the comparative safety of the Alle's right bank. Indeed, some accounts – including Wilson's – claim the Friedland bridges are fired by the retreating Bennigsen, obliging troops still trapped in town to scramble across a nearby ford: 'the bridges were ordered to be fired. The flames rolled over them instantaneously; they were no longer passable for friends or foes, and were consumed, notwithstanding the efforts of the enemy to preserve them, so that a great portion of the infantry were obliged to plunge into the stream and escape by an almost impracticable ford.'

Meanwhile, the forlorn and forsaken Gortchakov decides to act. Having failed in his assaults on Heinrichsdorf, the commander of Bennigsen's right-wing now faces an all-out assault by Lannes and Mortier, in accordance with Napoleon's plan. Ignorant that his line of retreat has been severed – and presumably receiving no orders from Bennigsen – Gortchakov turns about and heads for Friedland and the burning bridges over the Alle. Marbot continues:

> 'Up to this time Napoleon had, so to say, made his centre and left wing mark time. Now he pushed them rapidly forward. The Russian general, Gortchakov, who commanded the enemy's centre and right wing, obeying merely his own courage, wished to recapture the town. This would have been of no use to him, since the bridges were broken, but that he did not know. So he dashed forwards at the head of his troops into Friedland, blazing as it was: but repulsed in front by Ney's troops, who occupied the

town, and compelled to regain the open country, the enemy's general soon found himself surrounded by our centre, which pushed him back on the Alle … The Russians defended themselves with furious heroism, and though driven in on all sides refused to surrender. A large part fell under our bayonets, and the rest were rolled back from the top of the bank into the river, where nearly all were drowned.'

Marbot's account of the closing stages of the battle is echoed by Lejeune:

'All the Russian forces on the right of Friedland were driven back by Marshals Lannes and Mortier, and forced to retreat by way of the difficult fords of the Alle. Great numbers were drowned, and quantities of artillery and baggage were left embedded in the mud. Every house in the little town of Friedland was crowded with wounded Russians, and the reserve forces of the enemy made super human efforts to prevent our entering it. But we advanced all the same, and the fighting went on in the streets, which became literally choked with the bodies of men and horses killed by shot or bayonet. At last as the sun went down the French found themselves masters of the town, and with no more enemies to repulse.'

In the words of Jean Baptiste Barrès of the Guard: 'By ten o'clock at night the battle was won, the Russians driven in at all points and hurled into the Alle, the whole left bank being swept clean of them. Their losses were immense, in men and material both. This bloody and brilliant victory completely crushed them.' Having committed some 65,000 troops out of a total of 80,000 (the Imperial Guard and the bulk of I Corps seeing little action), Napoleon has finally achieved his battle of annihilation: handed to him on a plate by the luckless Bennigsen.

Russian losses are heavy, Bennigsen sustaining as many as 20,000 casualties: approximately one-third of his total force. According to de Norvins, entering town at the close of the action: 'we saw … all the bodies of the grenadiers of the Russian Guard still almost in line where they had fallen, and almost all with their wounds in the chest; that was as high as our soldiers could reach with the bayonet. Each of those brave men had defended and kept his station. The battle had lasted six hours.'

Friedland is a sorry sight, its narrow streets choked with bodies and abandoned equipment. Many corpses are half-consumed by fire, while trails of blood mark the fitful, convulsive movements of the wounded. Beyond town, the Russian dead lie in neat squares, indicating whole formations massacred by artillery. 'Pulverized by Napoleon's massed artillery fire,' writes historian, S.J. Watson, 'the Russians were finally swept away by the inexorable tide of Ney's advance.' And yet many have apparently been engulfed by the Alle, attempting to negotiate its waters following the destruction of the bridges. According to Jean-Roch Coignet of the Guard: 'The Russians fought like lions; they preferred to be drowned rather than to surrender.' French losses number perhaps 11,000.

As darkness falls, Bennigsen is already on the road to Wehlau with his survivors, covered by fire from those batteries which, unable to deploy in time for the battle, are still in tact on the right bank of the Alle. Napoleon sleeps on the battlefield. But first he dashes off a line to Josephine: 'The entire Russian Army is routed: eighty cannon, 30,000 men captured or killed, twenty-five Russian generals killed, wounded, or prisoners, the Russian Guard crushed … Do not worry and be happy.'

Napoleon's victory at Friedland is emphatic. Within the space of six hours, Bennigsen's army has been crippled, and effectively kicked out of Poland. But it has not been crushed, and there are some among the emperor's lieutenants who are dissatisfied: one general referring to Friedland as 'a battle gained and a victory lost.' The reason is that according to the military textbook, vanquished armies must be vigorously pursued to prevent them from rallying. To professional soldiers, the harrying of a beaten army is an accepted method of ensuring its complete destruction. In the wake of Jena and Auertädt, the French cavalry pursued the beaten Prussians mercilessly, maximizing battlefield successes by snuffing out the possibility of further resistance. But after Friedland the French cavalry remained passive. Even the Russian memoirist, Denis Davidov, noted that French operations after the battle were prosecuted, 'without notable enthusiasm'.

One reason put forward to explain the relative inactivity of the French post-Friedland is that the troops were exhausted by heat and hunger. Another is that there was some kind of breakdown in discipline, with many troops deserting the colours to pillage the local peasants. Both these arguments are valid enough, but a more tantalizing theory is offered by Petre, who observes that:

'A pursuit, such as that of the Prussians after Jena, must have caused the enemy much loss, and given rise to very bitter feelings towards the French … Napoleon did not wish to make a permanent enemy of Russia … He wanted Russia, as a sea power with a large seaboard and a great trade with England, to join him in his campaign against the commerce of his detested enemy. In these conditions, is it not probable that the emperor though that the destruction of a few thousand Russians, in a night pursuit, was not worth the risk of a continuation of the war?'

In other words, Petre is suggesting that having given the Russians a drubbing, Napoleon refrains from humiliating them further as a *beau geste* to the tsar. If true,

Campaign Chronicle

Petre's theory shows that even in the heat of victory, Napoleon is capable of replacing the instincts of a soldier for those of a diplomat.

Not that Napoleon's magnanimity – if indeed real – is appreciated by Bennigsen, who, having made it to Wehlau by 15 June, reflects on the events of the previous forty-eight hours:

> 'I freely admit that I should have done better not to undertake the affair of Friedland; I had the power, and I should have been safer to maintain my resolution, not to undertake a serious battle, since it was not necessary for the safety of the march of my army; but false reports, with which every general is often beset, had raised in me the erroneous view, which was confirmed by all my intelligence, that Napoleon had, with the greater part of his army, taken the road towards Königsberg …'

But in his official report to the tsar, Bennigsen keeps his chin up, imparting a liberal dose of spin to the Friedland fiasco:

> 'Although my loss, during a battle which lasted sixteen hours, and from my army's being obliged to file over a bridge, which was exposed to the enemy's artillery, cannot be inconsiderable, the enemy must have lost an equal number at least, from the attack with the bayonet, and of the cavalry charges; in the former of which we took from him the eagle of the 15th Regiment of the Line. Nor has the enemy taken any other prisoners but such as were wounded dangerously, and which could not be removed from the town, and only some dismounted pieces of cannon belonging to the regiments, with a few which could not be removed, because the horse attached to them had been shot. On the other hand, all our pieces of train artillery were got off safe. I am now taking with my army a position behind the Pregel, near Wehlau, causing all passes of that river, as far as Königsberg and Intersburg, to be occupied by my troops, in consequence whereof I have reopened a communication with General Lestocq. If the enemy should venture across the Pregel, I shall attack him immediately, and the reinforcements which already are on their march, will soon repair my loss, and enable me once more to contest with the enemy …'

But Bennigsen continues his retreat as the French finally mount a pursuit of sorts. According to Baron Boulart: 'On the 15th we pursued the Russians only to find that our passage over the Pregel at Wehlau was blocked owing to Bennigsen having destroyed the bridge. We had to make a bridge of boats and whilst it was being constructed we had a chance to sit and look over the beautiful Pregel valley. We had more need of sleep than splendid views, it is true, but it was too hot to sleep and there was no shade.' Meanwhile, Louis Lejeune is waylaid by local hospitality: 'the Germans, men and women alike, freed from the yoke of the Russians, who had treated them badly, received us with open arms …'

But at Königsberg French guns are bombarding the city. According to Petre, operations on 14 June came to a halt when Soult refused Murat's request to storm the city without artillery support. But by 3.00 p.m. on the 15th Soult's batteries are in place and the cannonade begins. Soult spends the rest of the day preparing his assault, perhaps with, perhaps without, the aid of his colleagues: some sources claiming Murat remains in overall command with Davout in support; others that Soult is alone before Königsberg, Murat and Davout having been recalled by Napoleon. Either way, by 10.00 p.m. on 15 June Soult is ready to crack open Königsberg. But Prussian deserters bring word that Kamenski has quit by the back door, and Lestocq will soon follow (Frederick William and his queen have already fled north-east to Memel). According to Petre – and most contemporary French reports – Soult enters town the following morning, finding the place crammed with wounded, ammunition, and all kinds of stores and supplies. An alternative version, however, flows from the pen of Sir Robert Wilson:

> 'On 17 June, at 4 o'clock at noon [sic], General Lestocq, having received advice of the Battle of Friedland, ordered the garrison under arms with the pretext of making a sally, but when the troops were all ready at their posts, he directed the columns out of Königsberg towards Labiau, leaving General Stutterheim, with two battalions of light infantry, to cover the retreat, who remained until midnight on the walls, when he retired, and on the morning of the 18th, the magistrates presented the keys to the enemy.'

Whatever the exact timetable, the result is the same: Königsberg falls following the Russian defeat at Friedland, leaving the French with the spoils of victory. Now all the Allied commanders – Bennigsen, Kamenski, Lestocq – are heading north-east for the border town of Tilsit on the River Niemen, followed at a fairly leisurely pace by a triumphant Napoleon.

16 June–9 July 1807: The Peace of Tilsit

Alexander is at Tilsit when news of Bennigsen's defeat breaks. With his army broken, Prussia prostrate, Sweden passive, and Britain generally unsupportive, the tsar wastes no time in drafting an armistice. The war is unpopular in Russia anyway, Alexander's mother – the formidable Maria Feodorovna – expressing the common view that Russian blood should no longer be spilled for the Hohenzollerns. Eager for peace, Alexander selects the courteous, diplomatic

Campaign Chronicle

Lieutenant General Lobanov-Rotovsky to bear his olive branch to Napoleon. Meanwhile, the lacklustre French pursuit continues, as described by de Gonneville:

> 'We followed the Russians, foot by foot, as far as Tilsit without encountering a serious resistance at any point. Only once towards evening they seemed to wish to make head, and it astonished us that the grand duke of Berg [Murat], who was there, was not so enterprising as the commander of the advance guard should be towards the rearguard of an army in retreat. At nightfall, without being pressed, he caused us to retire 2 leagues to take up a position in a large village upon a hill surrounded by several streams of water. Some pigs were found there and killed, but we had no bread or potatoes, and the hot pork without anything to eat with it, had a bad effect upon stomachs that had been empty so long …'

On 18 June, Lobanov-Rotovsky arrives at the French outposts. But the emperor has not yet arrived and Marshal Berthier – the commander on the spot – doubts the Russian's sincerity. To illustrate his contempt, Berthier keeps Lobanov

The Grand Duchy of Warsaw. Following the Peace of Tilsit, signed on 8 July 1807, Napoleon stripped Prussia of much of her Polish territory, to create the Grand Duchy of Warsaw, a French satellite under the nominal rule of his ally, the king of Saxony.

16 June–9 July 1807: The Peace of Tilsit

Marshal Soult (1769–1851). The capable leader of IV Corps, had a frustrating campaign, receiving a bloody nose at Eylau, and missing Friedland while attempting to take Königsberg.

waiting over an hour before receiving him. But the smooth and agreeable envoy keeps his cool and is permitted to await Napoleon's arrival next day.

Napoleon is secretly relieved to see Lobanov: his army needs respite just as much as Alexander's, being exhausted by hunger, heat, sickness and forced marches. Now he can see the final phase of his plan falling into place: Alexander wants peace. Alexander wants to talk. Very good: this is what the whole campaign has really been about. Time to launch the charm offensive …

Napoleon invites Lobanov to dinner, drinks a toast to the tsar's health, and suggests France and Russia are the rightful heirs to the European crown: France ruling in the West, Russia in the East. He calls for his maps and with Lobanov in attendance, fingers the line of the Vistula, naming it the natural boundary between the two empires. Lobanov is delighted – as Napoleon intended he

Napoleon and Alexander meet at Tilsit. The Polish gamble pays off, as Napoleon woos Alexander out of an alliance with Britain and into friendship with France. But the honeymoon would be short lived: three years later both emperors would be contemplating war.

should be – returning to Alexander with the welcome news that peace with France will not involve loss of territory or loss of face.

Meanwhile, the soldiers of the Grand Army form up before Tilsit on 19 June, fully expecting further bloodshed. De Gonneville continues:

'At last we arrived before Tilsit, and that was a sight I will endeavour to describe. The valley of the Niemen is commanded by a raised plateau on the side where we arrived. Tilsit was about half a league distant when we first perceived it, and we were formed up in order of battle … the Russian Army … [was] already on the opposite bank of the river, which is here of considerable size; they could easily be seen, some holding the positions assigned to them, some on the march to take up theirs. In front of Tilsit on our side, and all against the city, a corps of cavalry, composed of Cossacks, and intended to cover it, waiting till those still left in the town should have passed the wooden bridge that was already set on fire and had the last of the foot soldiers running over it as fast as they could. This cavalry seemed destined to be sacrificed by remaining behind, and had no course to pursue but to cross the river by swimming, an exercise the Cossacks in general are well accustomed to. All our remaining cavalry was almost on the spot gathered in a mass on the height …

'Our division on the right received orders to march on the enemy's cavalry before Tilsit. We began to move at a walk, in two lines of but small extent, in consequence of the losses we had experienced on the preceding days, especially the day of Heilsberg. There was something solemn in the movement we were executing. It was the last blow we were to strike, for the Russian Army, quite disorganised by successive defeats, had lost nearly all its artillery, and could not keep the field any longer, and the Prussians had not 10,000 men left. The last blow was to be delivered under the eyes of the emperor, as he could overlook the whole position, and under those of all the cavalry of the army, stationed so as not to lose the spectacle we were going to present. We understood this; an expression of pride could be seen on the faces of our cuirassiers; and though we were all so weak, no one had any doubts of success, as all felt a moral exaltation that supplied the place – and more – of physical power. We advanced in silence, and had nearly covered a quarter of the distance that divided us from the Russians, when an officer issued from their ranks, passed rapidly towards our ranks with a trumpeter, and raised one of his hands to show that he was carrying a paper … and in a few minutes an orderly officer of the emperor's came to us at full speed bringing an order to halt. It was peace …'

According to Baron Boulart: 'On the 19th the Russians had evacuated Prussian soil and recrossed the Niemen. We entered Tilsit, on the left bank of that river, the last Prussian town. We caught sight of the smoking ruins of the bridge which the Russians had burnt in order to put between us a barrier consisting of a wide, fast-flowing river.'

The French enter Tilsit in the rain. A number of fellow countrymen are discovered: prisoners of war who have been languishing in town for months. Most are suffering from tuberculosis. Meanwhile, the soldiers are hungry, but as usual there is no food, not even bread. Despite Lejeune's comment about being welcomed 'with open arms' by the local peasantry, it seems the people of Tilsit have buried their food, hoping the French will soon move on. When it becomes evident Napoleon will occupy the town for peace talks, the locals are obliged to dig up their eatables, surrendering a share to the soldiers.

Three days later, Napoleon issues a proclamation to his troops announcing the armistice:

> 'Soldiers, on 5 June we were attacked in our cantonments by the Russian Army, which misconstrued the causes of our inactivity. It perceived, too late, that our repose was that of the lion; now it does penance for its mistake. In the days of Guttstadt, of Heilsberg, in the ever-memorable days of Friedland, in ten days campaigning we have taken 120 guns, and seven standards; we have killed, wounded, or captured 60,000 Russians; torn from the enemy's army all its magazines, its hospitals, its ambulances, the fortress of Königsberg, the 300 vessels which were in port, laden with every kind of supplies, and 160,000 muskets, which England was sending to arm our enemies.
>
> 'From the shores of the Vistula, we have reached those of the Niemen, with the rapidity of the eagle. At Austerlitz you celebrated the anniversary of the coronation; you have this year worthily celebrated that of the Battle of Marengo, which put an end to the war of the Second Coalition. Frenchmen, you have been worthy of yourselves, and of me; you will return to France covered with laurels, after having acquired a peace which guarantees its own durability. It is time for our country to live in repose, sheltered from the malign influence of England.
>
> 'My rewards will prove to you my gratitude and the greatness of the love I bear you.'

But the weary soldiers – many now suffering from fever – are in a stupefied state of disbelief. Wandering around in a daze, they repeatedly ask each other: 'Is it true? Can it be true?'

On 24 June, Napoleon issues his 85th Bulletin at Tilsit, announcing more startling news:

> 'Tomorrow the two emperors of France and Russia are to have an interview. For this purpose a pavilion has been erected in the middle of the Niemen, to which the two monarchs will repair from each of its banks. Few sights will be more interesting. The two sides of the river will be lined by the two armies, while their chiefs confer on the means of re-establishing order, and giving repose to the existing generation.'

16 June–9 July 1807: The Peace of Tilsit

Meanwhile, Frederick William, hapless king of Prussia, has been summoned from Memel to hear his fate. As for Louise, his lovely but warlike queen, she is broken-hearted by defeat, and refuses to travel to Tilsit. Instead, she writes to Alexander, reminding him of former promises of friendship, and referring to him as the 'arbiter of our destiny'.

'The interview at Tilsit is one of the culminating points of modern history,' writes Bourrienne, 'and the waters of the Niemen reflected the image of Napoleon at the very height of his glory.' But the acme of Napoleon's campaign – indeed career –takes place not in a palace, nor on a battlefield, but on a raft, knocked together by French engineers within the space of eight hours. According to Savary, the imperial aide (whose brother was killed at the crossing of the Wkra back in December): 'The Emperor Napoleon … ordered a large raft to be floated in the middle of the river, upon which was constructed a room well covered in and elegantly decorated, having two doors on opposite sides, each of which opened into an ante-chamber. The roof was surmounted by two weathercocks: one displaying the eagle of Russia, and the other the eagle of France. The raft was precisely in the middle of the river.'

At 11.00 a.m. on 25 June, Alexander arrives at the riverside village of Picktupöhnen, looking suitably impressive in the dark green uniform of the Preobrajensky Guards. He is two hours early. He is also nervous. Napoleon, cleverly transforming statecraft into stagecraft, diplomacy into drama, has put the impressionable Alexander centre stage. Waiting in the wings is the tsar's ally, Frederick William, just arrived from Memel. Only two months ago, the two monarchs had signed a treaty of friendship, Alexander promising to guarantee Prussia's boundaries in any negotiated settlement with the French. Yet Frederick William – still king of Prussia and technically overlord at Tilsit – has been excluded from this first meeting. The French have not even bothered painting his monogram on their floating pavilion. It is clear this is a Franco–Russian show: but where does that leave Prussia …?

Eventually, shouts and acclamations herald Napoleon's arrival. He too is anxious. This is the moment he has been aiming for since the Polish campaign began. This is what his gamble has all been about. An ex-lieutenant of artillery, Napoleon has never entertained a monarch on equal terms before. Yet now he must eclipse Alexander, subdue him, overawe him, prise him out of Britain's arms and into his own.

The two emperors are rowed to the raft amid the cheers of their respective armies. Napoleon arrives first, welcoming Alexander aboard as his guest. The Russian – a tall man – towers over the Corsican, who is 5 foot 6 inches (1.67m) at most. They shake hands and disappear into the pavilion: two men, deciding the fate of a continent. Some sources claim Alexander's first words to Napoleon are: 'I hate the English as much as you do.' If so, Bonaparte must have heaved an immediate, if silent, sigh of relief. According to Savary: 'The two emperors met in the most amicable way. They remained together for a considerable time, and then took leave of each other with as friendly an air as that with which they had met.'

Napoleon and Alexander emerge after a discussion of some ninety minutes. Both men are smiling, and after agreeing to meet again next day, are rowed back to their respective banks of the river. But what has taken place? What have the two men decided?

It is clear Napoleon has completely won over Alexander, the two men apparently finding much common ground. In fact, both emperors desire peace, and are willing to sell their allies down the line to achieve it. For his part, Alexander is disillusioned with coalition partners Prussia, Sweden and Britain. He is ripe for a new guru, and immediately falls under the spell of Napoleon's charm and charisma. Transported with delight, Alexander returns from this first meeting in a state of childish glee. As the vanquished, he might reasonably have expected Napoleon, the victor, to exact a high price for peace: instead, Russia has been offered friendship, partnership, lasting tranquillity. Alexander is entranced, writing enthusiastic letters to family and friends describing Bonaparte in glowing terms.

As for Napoleon, he is delighted at Alexander's malleability. The Russian tsar is putty in his hands. After all the hardships, toils, blood and suffering of the winter campaign, Napoleon has emerged with peace on his terms. More importantly, he has emerged with a vision of Europe on his terms: a French-led empire committed to the cause of economic warfare with Britain. Thus the Polish gamble has paid-off big time. But it was never really about Poland. Sadly, Poland was just a means to an end: a way of reaching Russia, so to speak. And as Dabrowski's Poles cheer and yell their hearts out on the banks of the Niemen, they are applauding the triumph of French interests rather than Polish.

Next day, 26 June, Napoleon and Alexander resume talks. This time, Alexander asks if Frederick William might be included. Napoleon agrees, as a personal favour to his new-found friend. But Bonaparte makes a point of insulting Frederick William at every opportunity, making it clear he considers Prussia an old enemy and Russia a new ally. To emphasize this, Napoleon insists on negotiating separate treaties with Russia and Prussia. It is generally assumed Napoleon will punish Prussia severely for daring to make war on him.

Meanwhile, Tilsit is declared neutral territory and all three heads of state take up residence in town. Alexander arrives in Tilsit at 5.00 p.m. on 26 June, occupying one of the finer houses, protected by 800 soldiers of his Guard. According to Savary:

'On the day the Emperor Alexander entered Tilsit, the whole army was under arms. The Imperial Guard was drawn out in two lines of three deep from the landing-place to the Emperor Napoleon's quarters, and from thence to the quarters of the emperor of Russia. A salute of 100 guns was fired the moment Alexander stepped ashore, on the spot where the Emperor Napoleon was waiting to receive him. This meeting attracted visitors to Tilsit from 100 leagues round. M. de Talleyrand arrived, and after the observance of the usual ceremonies, business began to be discussed.'

In contrast, Frederick William is permitted to tag along, but receives no honours and is billeted in the house of a local miller. Traumatized, he writes to his wife, Louise, begging her to join him. Perhaps she can bring Alexander to his senses?

But the two emperors are on honeymoon, spending their time inspecting parades, riding in the country, taking tea and having dinner. To cement Franco–Russian relations, Napoleon orders his Imperial Guard to entertain their Russian counterparts. And so, with fever spreading through the rest French Army, a meal is prepared for the Russians in a nearby meadow, consisting of soup, meat and brandy. The preparations for, and the results of, these festivities are described by Jean-Roch Coignet:

'Orders were issued that we should prepare to give an entertainment to the Russian guard. Very long and wide tents were to be put up, with the openings all on a line, and with beautiful pine trees planted in front of them. One-half of us went with our officers to get the pine trees, and the other half put up the tents. Eight days were given us to make our preparations, and a circuit of 8 miles of country in which to procure provisions.

'We started off in good order, and that day the provisions were contracted for. The next day more than fifty waggons, loaded and driven by peasants, came to the camp. The peasants had conformed to this requisition with good grace, and they were sent off entirely satisfied. They thought that the carts, which were drawn by oxen, would be detained at the camp; but they were discharged immediately, and the peasants jumped for joy. At noon on 30 June, our feast was spread. More beautiful tables were never seen, all decorated with epergnes [i.e. an ornamental centrepiece for a dining table, usually holding fruit or flowers] made of turf, and filled with flowers. In the back part of each tent there were two stars with the names of the two great emperors formed of flowers, and draped with the French and Russian flags.

'We marched out in a body to meet this fine guard, which was to arrive by company. We each offered an arm to one of the giants, and as there were more of us than of them, we had one to every two of us. They were so tall they might have used us as walking canes. As for me, the smallest of all, I had one of them all to myself. I was obliged to look up to see his face. I looked like a little boy beside him. They were astonished to see us so splendidly dressed: even our cooks were all powdered, and wore white aprons to wait in. In fact, everything was in the best style.

'We seated our guests at table between us, and the dinner was well served. Everybody was in the highest spirits. These famished men could not control themselves; they did not know how to show the reserve which is proper at table. Brandy was served; it was the only liquor used at the entertainment. Before presenting it to them, we had to taste it, and then offer it in a tin goblet, which held a quarter of a litre. The contents of the goblet would instantly disappear. They would swallow pieces of meat as large as an egg at each mouthful. They seemed to become very uncomfortable. We made signs to them to unbutton their coats, doing the same thing ourselves. This made them easier. They had rags stuffed inside their uniforms to give them big chests, and it was disgusting to see these rags come tumbling out …'

At the beginning of July, Louise arrives at Tilsit. Sick, distraught, she cuts a tragic figure. Having helped ignite the war that ruined her husband, she has come to salvage his honour. Arriving in state mourning – a white crêpe dress – Louise's appearance brings forth gasps of appreciation from the assembled soldiery. Serene, sorrowful, bewitchingly beautiful, Louise has been instructed to use her charms to stop Bonaparte wiping Prussia off the map. Retention of the strategically important fortress of Magdeburg is seen as a particular objective.

Having joined Frederick William at the miller's house, Louise is visited by Napoleon on 6 July. He describes the meeting thus: 'She received me in tragic tones … "Sire! Justice! Magdeburg!" She went on in this fashion, which embarrassed me a good deal. Finally, to make her change, I asked her to be seated. Nothing is better suited for cutting a tragic scene short: once a person has sat down, it turns into comedy.'

But Napoleon is charmed and invites the Hohenzollerns to dinner. Louise is seated next to Napoleon, the soldiers of his Guard unable to avoid gawping at the captivating queen. Napoleon offers Louise a red rose, but she refuses to accept it, coyly announcing she would rather have Magdeburg. Napoleon is immune to this kind of coquetry, haughtily informing Louise it is for him to give and her to receive. But the dinner passes off pleasingly enough, Napoleon asking the queen and her husband to dine the following evening. Prussian hopes are raised.

But next day Napoleon and Alexander sign the Treaty of Tilsit and the extent of Franco–Russian collaboration becomes apparent. With Frederick William due to sign a separate accord two days later, Louise is heartbroken. She refuses to dine with Napoleon at first, but eventually relenting, suffers a public humiliation with subdued dignity. At one point, the *beau sabreur* Murat – ignoring court etiquette – sidles up to the Prussian queen to ask how she passes her spare time? When Louise answers that she reads history, Murat observes it might be more profitable to study current affairs …

By 9 July it's all over and Napoleon is on his way back to Paris, having punished Prussia for refusing his friendship and making war on him; partly rewarded the Poles by granting them a small, semi-autonomous state (run on French lines, with a French representative in Warsaw calling the shots, and under the nominal rule of the king of Saxony); abandoned his former ally Turkey as a concession to Alexander; and succeeded in isolating Britain from Europe – politically, militarily, economically – by cementing a new friendship with Russia. Petre sums up the terms of the treaties:

'Napoleon, bent on passing every possible insult upon the unfortunate Prussians, attributed such poor terms as he granted them to the intercession of Alexander. Of the conquered territories, he restored to Prussia that part of the Duchy of Magdeburg which was situated on the right bank of the Elbe, thereby excluding the fortress itself, which he knew the queen specially cherished. Also he surrendered Pomerania, Silesia, and other territories constituting approximately the kingdom as it was before 1 January 1772. From that portion of the ancient kingdom of Poland which had been acquired by Prussia in and after 1772 he constituted the Grand Duchy of Warsaw, which he presented to the king of Saxony, together with a military right of way across the intervening Prussian territory. He excepted a considerable area in the direction of Bialystok, which was made over to Russia. Danzig he made a free city, under the protection of Prussia and Saxony. The recognition of the Napoleonic kingdoms of Naples and Holland, of the Confederation of the Rhine, of the new kingdom of Westphalia, now carved out of Prussian territory west of the Elbe and bestowed on Jérôme Bonaparte, was stipulated for. Turkey, which had so materially helped him, was abandoned by Napoleon, anxious in every way to conciliate Russia. He merely offered his mediation between the two powers, whilst agreeing to accept that of the tsar between England and himself. Prussia, as well as Russia, were bound to aid his campaign against the commerce of Great Britain.'

Aftermath

——◦•(•)•◦——

'With so many battles fought, so many victories won, so many obstacles overcome, and the triumphs of the diplomat added to those of the general … Napoleon re-entered his capital on the 27th of July … This return was celebrated by public holidays, glittering with civil, military and religious display.' This is how Chancellor Pasquier describes Napoleon's homecoming on 27 July 1807. He has returned from Poland the most powerful man in the world. Furthermore, his vision of Europe has gained weight with Alexander's apparent willingness to bind Russia's fortunes to those of France. Seemingly, at last, Napoleon has not only won the war, he has won the peace. As *de facto* emperor of Europe, surely Napoleon's throne is secure? Pasquier continues:

> 'I seem to see him now, as he was that day in his garb of state, which, though slightly theatrical, was yet beautiful and noble. His features, always composed and grave, put one in mind of the cameos representing the Roman emperors. He was a small man, and yet his whole person, in that impressive ceremony, matched the role he had to sustain. The habit of command and the sense of his might increased his stature. A sword sparkling with gems hung at his side; the famous diamond known as the Regent formed the pommel of it. Its brilliance did not suffer one to forget that that sword was the heaviest and most triumphant the world had seen since those of Alexander and Caesar. I recall that M. Beugnot, who was sitting next me, made the remark. Both of us were then far from dreaming that less than seven years would suffice to break it …'

And yet by 1814 Napoleon had been toppled from power. The seventh anniversary of the Treaty of Tilsit saw him in exile at Elba, following abdication and a botched suicide attempt. The emperor could not have known it at the time, but his road to ruin actually began at Tilsit, as the ink was drying on the treaties concluded with his vanquished enemies, Russia and Prussia.

Aftermath

Napoleon's achievement at Tilsit appears to represent a 'good day at the office' by any standards. Ten years after the event, in final exile on St Helena, the fallen emperor recalled it as one of the happiest times of his life: 'suddenly I found myself victorious, laying down the law, courted by emperors and kings …'

But if Tilsit represents the flower of Napoleon's ambition, its seeds produced his downfall. Even at the time, there were some among the emperor's circle who believed he had punished Prussia too severely. While others wondered if enough common ground really existed between France and Russia to ensure a lasting peace. Subsequent events would prove such fears well-founded.

As far as Prussia was concerned, Napoleon only refrained from dethroning Frederick William as a gesture to Alexander. At Tilsit, Bonaparte would have gladly snapped Prussia like a straw: but the desire for good relations with Alexander pulled him back from the brink. And so, although retaining its status as an independent kingdom, Prussia was shorn of half its territory. Russia was presented with the eastern Bialystok region of Poland, while lands west of the Elbe were filched to create Westphalia: a new kingdom for Napoleon's kid brother, Jérôme. Much of Prussia's eighteenth century Polish acquisitions were transformed into a puppet-state, the Grand Duchy of Warsaw. Prussia was then saddled with a war indemnity of 120 million francs, and occupied by French troops until it was paid off. But such an enormous sum could not be raised easily: land had to be sold, property too; loans had to be secured, and taxes raised from 10 to 30 per cent. To make matters worse, forced membership of the Continental System curtailed trade, plunging ordinary Prussians into the economic mire, and unleashing a spate of bankruptcies. But the privations endured by Prussia as a result of Napoleon's malice merely fuelled an all-consuming desire for revenge …

In Russia, too, economic depression followed entry into the Continental System. Britain was Russia's main export customer, and though Alexander had cause to be disillusioned with London (which had offered little direct military aid during the war with Napoleon, while making it clear Russian expansion in the Balkans and Mediterranean would not be tolerated), the severing of trade links brought the country to the brink of ruin. Meanwhile, the transformation of the Grand Duchy of Warsaw into an armed camp, complete with a Polish Army under Prince Poniatowski (nephew of Stanislaw II, the last king of Poland), alarmed St Petersburg to such an extent that by 1810 Napoleon and Alexander were on a collision course once again.

War would not kick off again until 1812, but when it came, it brought an avalanche of catastrophes on Napoleon's head. Alexander's victory in 1812 encouraged Prussia to shake off its shackles, and by 1813 Europe was ablaze with the War of German Liberation. Napoleon was evicted from Germany and in 1814 a new coalition – consisting of Austria, Britain, Prussia and Russia –

Napoleon's Polish Gamble

successfully invaded France. Finally defeated at Waterloo – largely thanks to the efforts of a Prussian army under the fanatical French-hater Marshal Blücher – Napoleon was left with nothing but his regrets: 'I committed three great political faults: I ought to have made peace with England in abandoning Spain; I ought to have restored the kingdom of Poland; and not to have gone to Moscow ...'

As for the Poles, who fought so hard for the triumph at Tilsit, they remained faithful to Napoleon till the last. Grateful for a whiff of freedom, in the form of the Grand Duchy of Warsaw, the Polish patriots remained convinced that eventually Napoleon would restore the whole kingdom.

But the Grand Duchy of Warsaw was little more than a recruiting ground for the Grand Army. Reclaimed from land grabbed by Prussia in the eighteenth century (principally Mazovia and Wielkpolska), it was organized into six departments: Warsaw, Kalisz, Poznan, Bydgoszcz, Plock, and Lomza. Run on French lines – complete with a constitution, granted by Napoleon on 22 July 1807 – the duchy was placed under the nominal rule of King Frederick August III of Saxony. In reality, however, the duchy was a puppet-state, with a French representative at Warsaw overseeing affairs. Although created grand duke, Frederick August ruled 'under the Protector of the Rhine' – i.e. Napoleon. But the Poles did get their own army, led by blue-blooded Jozef Poniatowski: much to the hard-fighting Dabrowski's *chagrin*. Despite further territorial additions at Austria's expense in 1809, the Grand Duchy of Warsaw was doomed to extinction following Napoleon's reverses in 1812–13. By the time the Napoleonic Wars ended in 1815, Russian troops were back in Warsaw. The clock was then turned back to 1795 and the days of the Third Partition. Although Krakow was granted a measure of autonomy as a city-state, Poland would not emerge as an independent nation until 1918.

And yet Poland changed Napoleon's life and arguably the fate of Europe. For Marie Walewska bore Napoleon a son in 1810. Prior to this, the emperor had thought himself infertile. Dreaming of a Bonaparte dynasty ruling Europe for generations, Napoleon promptly divorced the obviously infertile Josephine – his 'Lucky Star' – to hook up with a Habsburg princess. Meanwhile, making do with a bit part in the emperor's life, and with little chance of improving her status, Marie Walewska remained faithful to the last: embodying Poland's relationship with Napoleonic France. For it is sad to relate that those Poles who took up arms for France – fighting 'for your freedom and ours' – were merely pawns in a bigger game, as the following lines, scribbled in Napoleon's hand on a draft statement dated May 1807, clearly show: 'Do not mention Polish indpependence and suppress everything tending to show the emperor as the liberator of Poland, seeing that he has never explained himself of that subject ...'

Biographical Notes

※※※

The French
Augereau, Marshal Pierre François Charles, duc de Castiglione (1757–1816). Uneducated, coarse, brutal, Augereau commanded VII Corps until invalided home after Eylau in February 1807. A Parisian of humble origins, Augereau was a one-time duellist, deserter, and dancing-master. But his fortunes were fast-tracked thanks to the Revolution, and by 1796 he was serving as a general in Bonaparte's Army of Italy. One of the original marshals created in 1804, Augereau was not a Napoleon-lover, eventually falling out of favour for daring to criticize the emperor's generalship. According to Petre, Augereau's intelligence 'was not great, his education very little; yet he maintained discipline among his men, and was beloved by them.'

Bernadotte, Marshal Jean-Baptiste-Jules (1763–1844). Poised, polished, ambitious, Bernadotte commanded I Corps until wounded at Spanden in June 1807. An ex-sergeant major who rose to the rank of general, Bernadotte was linked to the Bonaparte clan by marriage, wedding Joseph Bonaparte's sister-in-law in 1798. Nevertheless, he was a political rival of Napoleon's, their relationship being an uneasy one. Made a marshal in 1804, Bernadotte fell out of favour in 1806, for refusing to aid Davout at the Battle of Auerstädt. Napoleon considered trying Bernadotte for treason – or incompetence – but let the matter pass for 'personal reasons.' Interestingly, Bernadotte's humane treatment of Swedish prisoners – caught up in the campaign of 1806–07 defending Swedish Pomerania – would result in his being elected crown prince of Sweden in 1810. He ascended the throne as Charles XIV in 1818, and his descendants rule to this day. According to Petre, Bernadotte was: 'Calm, selfish, calculating, and astute, of much more polished manners than most of Napoleon's marshals, he was endowed with considerable powers of command.'

Berthier, Marshal Louis-Alexandre (1753–1815). An ex-engineer in the Royalist Army, Berthier became Napoleon's chief of staff in 1796, initiating a perfect military partnership. According to the historian, Foord, Berthier's 'methodical habits and untiring industry, coupled with his complete familiarity with Napoleon's character, rendered him indispensable to the latter. His military talents were not remarkable, and his general position was rather that of a confidential secretary than that of a modern chief of staff.' Napoleon recognized Berthier's limitations as a battlefield commander, but equally, his talents as an administrator. According to Petre, Berthier was 'an ideal chief of the staff. He was no general … but he knew Napoleon, his ways and his wishes, and could elaborate, to the liking of his master, the brief orders which were what he usually received.'

Bessières, Marshal Jean-Baptiste (1768–1813). An ex-grenadier in Louis XVI's Guard, who defended the Tuileries on 10 August 1792 against the Paris Mob, Bessières became one of Napoleon's most devoted lieutenants. Made a marshal in 1804, he commanded the cavalry of the emperor's Imperial Guard. According to Petre, Bessières 'was not in the first rank amongst the marshals, and acting, as he generally did, under the personal command of Napoleon, he had no special opportunity for establishing a reputation for originality or independence.'

Bonaparte, Jérôme (1784–1860). The youngest and perhaps least talented of the Bonaparte brothers, whose reputation is largely based on his extravagant lifestyle and playboy antics. Jérôme's bravery was never in doubt, but he lacked experience as a leader, and when given command of IX Corps, largely relied on Vandamme, one of his divisional generals. Napoleon made Jérôme king of newly-created Westphalia in July 1807: he brought it to the brink of ruin and revolution within two years.

Davout, Marshal Louis Nicholas (1770–1823). An ex-cavalry officer with an aristocratic background, Davout commanded III Corps – perhaps the best unit in the Grand Army. A veteran of Bonaparte's Egyptian campaign, Davout was made a marshal in 1804. He won a famous victory at Auerstädt in 1806, smashing the bulk of the Prussian Army single-handed. According to the historian, Foord, Davout was 'a fine example of the modern scientific soldier, a stern disciplinarian and an admirable administrator, with a passion for order and method.' His love of discipline earned him the nickname of 'the Iron Marshal', and yet, as Petre observes, Davout was 'apparently popular with his men and subordinates.'

Lannes, Marshal Jean (1769–1809). Highly esteemed by Napoleon, and the only marshal to be on familiar terms with the emperor. A man of little formal education, Lannes was a student of war, and commanded V Corps until wounded at Pultusk in December 1806. He returned to duty in spring 1807 at the head of a 'Reserve Army', which saw service at Danzig, Heilsberg and Friedland. According to Petre, Lannes was 'Impetuous, and ever ready to throw himself into the thickest of the fray … and on more than one occasion in the Polish campaign he fought a good and patient battle against very superior numbers. He feared neither the enemy nor the emperor.'

Marshal François-Joseph Lefebvre (1755–1820). The son of a miller, Lefebvre enlisted in 1773, rising to the rank of sergeant by the time revolution broke out in 1789. Four year later, he was a general. One of the original marshals created in 1804, Lefebvre commanded the infantry of the Imperial Guard in 1806, before taking command of X Corps in January 1807. His capture of Danzig in May 1807 arguably won the war for Napoleon, and he was rewarded with a dukedom. A simple, honest soldier, Lefebvre married a laundry-woman in 1783 and remained devoted to her. Despite wealth and titles, neither Lefebvre nor his wife, Catherine, attempted to polish their manners or modify their accents, gaining for them a curious mixture of ridicule and respect.

Masséna, Marshal André (1758–1817). Rumoured to be of Jewish origin, Masséna was orphaned as a boy and raised by his uncle, before enlisting in 1775. A hero of the Revolutionary Wars, dubbed the 'Spoilt Child of Victory', Masséna became one of Napoleon's ablest and most trusted subordinates. Summoned to Poland from Italy in the spring of 1807, Masséna was given command of V Corps, and ordered to defend Warsaw. He would see little action, but managed to contract a lung complaint, and would spend almost a year on sick leave. According to Petre, Masséna was 'the most brilliant of the marshals, and the best fitted for the command of an army.'

Mortier, Marshal Edouard-Adolphe-Casimir-Joseph (1768–1835). The half-English son of a merchant, Mortier enlisted in the wake of the Revolution. A gifted administrator, he was made a marshal in 1804, becoming one of Napoleon's most loyal supporters. In the campaign of 1806–07 Mortier led VIII Corps, seeing action in Pomerania and at Friedland. According to Petre, Mortier was 'a general of average capacity, good enough for the command of a corps, hardly suited for independent command of an army.'

Murat, Marshal Joachim, grand duke of Berg (1767–1815). The ambitious, flamboyant, charismatic brother-in-law to the emperor (he married Caroline Bonaparte in 1800) who commanded the Cavalry Reserve. Murat adopted Polish costume for the campaign, vainly seeing himself as future king of a reconstituted Poland. Riding into battle armed only with a jewelled riding crop, Murat's charge at Eylau probably saved Napoleon's skin. His performance at Heilsberg, however, was poor, earning a reprimand from Napoleon. An inspiring leader, Murat was ignorant of the basics of good cavalry command, caring little for the welfare of his men and horses.

Napoleon I (1769–1821). Suffice it to say that by 1806 Napoleon's reputation as the greatest captain of his age was truly established. The conqueror of Italy and Egypt, the victor of Austerlitz and Jena, his genius for war was unrivalled. A master strategist and tireless worker, Napoleon's spectacular career was guided by his own fascination with Classical civilization and the achievements of Alexander the Great and Julius Caesar. An ex-artillery officer and Republican hero, Napoleon crowned himself emperor of the French in 1804, creating an imperial vision that would finally crash eleven years later at Waterloo.

Ney, Marshal Michel (1769–1815). The son of a barrel-maker from Saarlouis, the red-haired Ney enlisted as a hussar trooper in 1787. The Revolution kick-started his career, however, and by 1799 Ney was a general of division. Made a marshal in 1804, Ney gained fame as the brave, dogged – and occasionally insubordinate – leader of VI Corps. According to Petre, Ney 'was at his best commanding the rearguard of a retreating army … In the front, or detached, he seemed to lose his head, would be carried away by ambitious projects, and sometimes run great and unnecessary risk, almost in defiance of orders.' While Foord states that Ney: 'was a fine tactician, and as a corps commander probably unsurpassed.'

Soult, Marshal Nicolas Jean-de-Dieu (1769–1851). The son of a notary, Soult enlisted in 1785, becoming a general of division in 1799. Made a marshal in 1804, Soult rivals Davout and Masséna as Napoleon's most capable commander. Distinguished at Austerlitz and Jena, his IV Corps was hard-pressed at Eylau, and missed Friedland altogether, being occupied with the seizure of Königsberg. According to Petre, Soult was 'beyond doubt, a capable commander.'

Victor, General (later Marshal) Claude (1764–1841). Of humble background, Victor enlisted in the artillery in 1781. Sixteen years later, he was a general of division, and in 1806 was chief of staff to Lannes. Earmarked to lead X Corps, Victor was captured in January 1807, though released in time to take charge of the Siege of Graudenz in May 1807. He replaced Bernadotte at the head of I Corps in June, serving with distinction at Friedland, and being made a marshal shortly after (13 July 1807).

Biographical Notes

The Allies

Alexander I (1777–1825). Succeeded his murdered – and apparently mad – father, Paul I on 24 March 1801. Initially fascinated by Napoleon, Alexander was appalled by the execution of the duc d'Enghien in 1805. Promptly taking Russia to war with France, Alexander and his Austrian allies were defeated at Austerlitz on 2 December 1805. Returning to the fight in 1806 – this time in support of Prussia – Alexander dumped his coalition partners in favour of friendship with France, following defeat at Friedland. But cooperation with Napoleon was shortlived: by 1810 Alexander was contemplating yet another shift of allegiance, creating a diplomatic crisis leading to the French invasion of Russia in 1812.

Bagration, General Peter (1765–1812). A Georgian prince who had served under the legendary Suvorov, Bagration joined Bennigsen's force in 1807, following Buxhöwden's return to Russia. A fiery character adored by his men, Bagration took command of Bennigsen's rearguard, serving with great distinction. According to Foord, 'Bagration was essentially a fighter: his tactics were usually influenced by his combative instincts; and his excitable temperament rendered him reckless of his person.' For some, Bagration was a 'Russian Murat'.

Barclay de Tolly, Mikhail Andreas (1761–1818). A Livonian of Scots ancestry, Barclay's rise had, in the words of Foord, 'been very slow, owing to his unassuming character and to lack of influence.' By 1806, however, Barclay was a lieutenant general, and according to Petre, he 'greatly distinguished himself in this campaign, in command of a division, especially at Eylau.' Best known for his defence of the Motherland in the war of 1812, Foord notes that for Barclay, 'Patriotism and devotion to duty were to him a religion.'

Bennigsen, General Count Levin A.T. (1745–1826). A Hanoverian who entered Russian service in 1773, Bennigsen began the campaign in command of the tsar's First Army. Following Marshal Kamenskoi's resignation in December 1806, Bennigsen became commander-in-chief, following his alleged 'victory' at Pultusk. According to Petre, Bennigsen 'can hardly be described as a great general.' And yet he consistently escaped Napoleon's well-prepared traps, and fought the emperor to a standstill at Eylau. But his failure to relieve Danzig, followed by an ill-conceived and ill-coordinated spring offensive, put ultimate victory out of reach. By the end of the campaign, Bennigsen – dogged by ill-health and poor relations with subordinates – had run out of options. Falling into a trap of his own making at Friedland, Bennigsen's reputation was among the casualties of his defeated army.

Napoleon's Polish Gamble

Buxhöwden, Lieutenant General Friedrich Wilhelm, count (1750–1811). An Estonian German who married an illegitimate daughter of Catherine the Great, Buxhöwden was a veteran of Suvorov's campaigns in Poland (1793–94), and an ex-governor of the tsar's Polish territories. A bitter rival of Bennigsen's – to whom he was officially superior – Buxhöwden began the campaign as commander the tsar's Second Army. He briefly held the command-in-chief – following Kamenskoi's sudden retirement on 28 December 1806 – but was obliged to give it up to Bennigsen, the 'victor' of Pultusk. Buxhöwden quit the army and went home on 14 January 1807.

Frederick William III (1770–1840). The son of Frederick William II and great-nephew of Frederick the Great. A liberal-minded monarch who lifted many repressive measures, this pacifist king was forced into war with Napoleon against his better judgement. After the annihilation of his field army at Jena–Auerstädt on 14 October 1806, Frederick William fled to East Prussia, seeking the support of Tsar Alexander. According to Napoleon, Frederick William 'was a tall, dry-looking fellow and would give a good idea of Don Quixote. He attached more importance to the cut of a dragoon or a hussar uniform than would have been necessary for the salvation of a kingdom.'

Gallitzin, Prince Andrei (dates unknown). Petre dismisses Gallitzin's service in 1806–07 with the words: 'led the Russian cavalry with ability'. But the general earned high praise from Napoleon for his impressive performance at Golymin on 26 December 1806, in which he fended off repeated attacks and made good his escape against overwhelming odds. Gallitzin was present at Eylau and Friedland, commanding Bennigsen's cavalry with distinction before apparently disappearing into obscurity.

Kalkreuth, Friedrich Adolf, Count von, (1737–1818). Also spelt 'Kalreuth', 'Kalckreuth' and Kalruth', this Prussian general had been aide-de-camp to Frederick the Great's brother, Prince Henry. A distinguished veteran of the Seven Years War, Kalkreuth commanded the Prussian Reserve Corps in 1806, covering the retreat from Auerstädt. Best known for his 78-day defence of Danzig in 1807, he was later promoted field marshal, and conducted Prussia's peace negotiations at Tilsit. According to Petre, Kalkreuth 'had seen much of war … He was, however, at times wanting in resolution and perseverance.'

Kamenskoi, Marshal Alexander (1731–1807). Not to be confused with General Kamenski (spelt 'Kamenskoi' in some sources), leader of the abortive attempt to relieve Danzig by sea, Kamenskoi was the tsar's original commander-in-chief in Poland. Unfit for high command, this superannuated veteran received his posting on 7 December 1806 and quit three weeks later. He was replaced first by Buxhöwden and then Bennigsen. According to Petre, Kamenskoi 'was now too old for war … His violent character, which eventually led to his assassination by a peasant, rendered him unsuitable for supreme command.'

Lestocq, General Anton (dates unknown). The General in command of a Prussian corps, which, as the nation's only remaining field force, operated in conjunction with the Russian Army. According to F.D. Logan: 'Lestoq gained for himself a great reputation in this war, and proved himself a worthy opponent of the famous marshals of France.' Lestocq's most notable feat was the march to Eylau in support of Bennigsen's hard-pressed army, described by Petre as 'a masterpiece of patience and resolution.'

Platov, General Matvei Ivanovich (1751–1818). One of the period's most colourful commanders, Platov found fame as the leader of the Don Cossacks, becoming their *hetman* in 1801. According to Foord, Platov 'was a burly, genial officer, uniting to considerable military talents the daring and good humour which were even more important in the eyes of his wild followers.' While Petre states that, as leader of the Cossacks, Platov's 'example would rally them against fearful odds. He had only to dismount and call upon his horsemen in order to stop the spread of disorder.'

Orders of Battle

It is a feature of the 'Campaign Chronicles' series to give detailed orders of battle where known. Such lists, illustrating the command structure of armies and unit strengths, are useful aids when attempting to understand or recreate a military action. But in the present volume, I feel unable to provide such a helpful piece of apparatus.

Having consulted many books on Napoleon's Polish campaign, I am daunted by the inconsistencies of published sources regarding orders of battle. Readers keen to study this aspect of the campaign are therefore directed to works such as Wilson's *Brief Remarks on the Character and Composition of the Russian Army, and a Sketch of the Campaigns in Poland in the Years 1806 and 1807*, Foucart's *Campagne du Pologne*, Höpfner's *Der Krieg von 1806 und 1807*, Nafziger's *The Eylau–Friedland Campaign of 1807–07*, and Digby Smith's *Napoleonic Wars Data Book*. I would also like to recommend excellent articles by Tony Broughton and Stephen Millar on the 'Napoleon Series' website (www.napoleon-series.org).

Yet it must be stated that scholars and aficionados are wary of announcing definitive orders of battle for Napoleon's Polish campaign. According to Petre: 'it is only possible by a comparison of the different authorities to arrive at an approximation of the truth.' While George F. Nafziger writes that: 'The precise organization of the armies at Eylau are a question [sic] that has never been answered. No documents … have, to date, been found that document the strengths and organizations [sic] of the two armies upon the day of battle.' Meanwhile, Stephen Millar, in an article posted on the 'Napoleon Series' website, writes: 'Bennigsen's army at Eylau has one of the more confusing orders of battle of the Napoleonic Wars … Organizational sources often conflict with each other.' Millar goes on to suggest that published sources are at best 'uncertain', sealing his argument by pointing out that contemporary estimates of Bennigsen's strength at Eylau range from 63,000 to 80,000.

Perhaps, at a distance of 200 years, it is not unreasonable that organizational details of the rival armies are unclear. After all, huge numbers of men were involved, and operations conducted in the usual 'fog of war', with commanders giving no thought to the needs of future historians. And yet, it is possible that even at the time, the picture regarding unit strengths and organization was sketchy at best. Napoleon used such information as a weapon to confuse his enemies, distorting troop returns and casualty figures for effect. His subordinates, too, were not above massaging the figures, in order to escape the emperor's wrath. For example, the memoirist, Marbot, writes: 'The emperor used as a rule to treat his officers with kindness, but there was one point on which he was, perhaps, over severe. He held the colonels responsible for maintaining a full complement of men in the ranks of their regiments, and as that is precisely what is most difficult to achieve on a campaign, it was just on this point that the emperor was most often deceived.' A similar situation no doubt existed in rival armies, with commanders like Bennigsen answerable to higher authorities – unlike Napoleon, who was head of state as well as commander-in-chief.

And so it is possible that much of the time, contemporary commanders were forced to rely on what they could actually see with their own two eyes: the 'little picture'. Conversely – removed in time and with the benefit of hindsight – it is we who are left with the 'big picture': but as Petre states, this can only be 'an approximation of the truth'.

Roll Call

The human cost of Napoleon's Polish campaign is difficult to asses. The fact is, no one really knows how many soldiers and civilians were killed, let alone wounded or made sick. What can be stated is that by the formal end of operations in July 1807 Polish hospitals were crammed with 27,000 French troops: 53 per cent being fever cases, 24 per cent battlefield casualties, 16 per cent venereal patients, and 7 per cent scurvy sufferers.

Despite Napoleon's assertion that 'Absolute power has no need to lie', his army bulletins almost always distorted information – including casualty figures – for public consumption. Serving as his own propagandist, Napoleon made 'spin' a feature of his government, admitting to his brother Joseph: 'Newspapers are not history any more than bulletins are history.' Indeed, the emperor's army had a saying: 'to lie like a bulletin'.

But even if proffered in good faith, contemporary casualty figures are misleading. For example: 'wounded' troops might be patched up and sent back into action almost immediately; 'sick' troops might recover; 'captured' troops might be released or exchanged; and 'missing' troops might miraculously reappear soon after battle. Indeed, thousands of troops went 'missing' in Poland, but most were simply looking for food.

All that can be said is the Grand Army suffered fewer casualties than the combined total of its Prussian and Russian enemies, perhaps by as much as 50 per cent.

Campaign Glossary

ADC/Aide-de-Camp: an officer on the staff of a general, primarily used for delivering orders and dispatches, and making eyewitness reports.

Caisson: a four-wheeled ammunition waggon.

Carabiniers: 'heavy' cavalrymen armed with short-barrelled muskets called *carabines* (carbines).

Case Shot: a kind of artillery projectile (also referred to as 'canister'), consisting of a tin case packed with bullets. When fired, the case would rupture, scattering the bullets over a wide area.

Chasseurs á Cheval: 'light' cavalrymen, used for reconnaissance, skirmishing and outposts duties.

Chasseurs á Pied: 'light' infantrymen trained to fight as skirmishers.

Cossacks: irregular cavalrymen in the service of the tsar.

Cuirassiers: 'heavy' cavalrymen protected by 'cuirasses' – metal body-armour front and back.

Defile: an obstacle or narrow space that forces marching troops into a column in order to pass.

Division: a body of troops, usually several thousand strong, supported by guns.

Dragoons: 'medium' cavalry, often armed with muskets, trained to fight on horseback or on foot.

Eagle: regimental standards presented by Napoleon, based on the imperial eagle of Ancient Rome, and designed by Chaudet in 1804.

Gendarmes: mounted bodyguards or military police.

Grenadier: picked infantrymen, selected for height and strength, and deployed as shock troops. Originally armed with grenades, hence the name.

Howitzer: a short-barrelled artillery piece used for high-trajectory firing.

Hussars: 'light' cavalrymen based on the Hungarian irregulars of the eighteenth century. Piratical – or perhaps theatrical – in appearance, hussars were used for scouting, raiding, etc.

Jäger: a German term for a 'light' infantryman or skirmisher.

Line of Communication: the link between an army on campaign and its source of supply.

Magazine: a depot or ammunition store.

Musketeers: line infantry armed with muskets.

Outpost: a lookout or sentry-post.

Parallel: a trench dug 'parallel' to the walls of a besieged city.

Sap: communication trenches linking 'parallels' (see above).

Sapper: a private soldier in the Engineers.

Tirailleurs: 'light' infantrymen trained as marksmen or riflemen.

Voltigeurs: 'light' infantrymen, supposedly agile enough to keep pace with a trotting horse.

Appendix

Appendix: German Place Names and their Polish/Lithuanian/Russian Equivalents

Please note: names marked with an asterisk indicate places in the present-day Russian enclave of Kaliningrad. Those marked with a double asterisk are in present-day Lithuania. Otherwise, all names listed are in the present-day Republic of Poland.

Alle, river (Łyna, river)
Allenstein (Olsztyn)
Bartenstein (Bartoszyce)
Bischofsburg (Biskupiec)
Braunsberg (Braniewo)
Breslau (Wrocław)
Brieg (Brzeg)
Bromberg (Bydgoszcz)
Danzig (Gdańsk)
Deppen (Mostkowo)
Dirschau (Tczew)
Domnau (Domnovo)*
Elbing (Elbląg)
Eylau (see Preussisch-Eylau)
Frauenburg (Frombork)
Freystadt (Kożuchów)
Friedland (Pravdinsk)*
Glatz (Kłodzko)
Glogau (Głogów)
Graudenz (Grudziądz)
Guttstadt (Dobre Miasto)
Heilsberg (Lidzbark Warmiński)
Insterburg (Tschernjachovsk)*
Jenkendorf (Jonkowo)
Johannisburg (Pisz)
Johannisburg Forest (Puszcza Piska)
Kahlberg (Krynica Morska)
Kolberg (Kołobrzeg)
Kosel (Kozle)

Kreuzburg (Kluczbork)
Labiau (Polessk)*
Landsberg (Górowo Iławeckie)
Lautenburg (Lidzbark Welski)
Marienburg (Malbork)
Marienwerder (Kwidzyn)
Mehlsack (Pieniężno)
Memel (Klaipeda)**
Mewe (Gniew)
Mohrungen (Morąg)
Neidenburg (Nidzica)
Neisse (Nysa)
Oder, river (Odra, river)
Passarge, river (Pasłęka, river)
Passenheim (Pasym)
Persante, river (Parsęta)
Posen (Poznań)
Pregel, river (Pregolja, river)*
Preussisch-Eylau (Bagrationovsk)*
Schweidnitz (Świdnica)
Soldau (Działdowo)
Stettin (Szczecin)
Tapiau (Gvardeysk)*
Thorn (Toruń)
Tilsit (Sovietsk)*
Vistula, river (Wisła, river)
Waltersdorf (Wilczkowo)
Wormditt (Orneta)

Bibliography

The following books were consulted in the preparation of this volume, and I am indebted to their authors, editors and translators.

Atteridge, A.H., *Marshal Murât, King of Naples*, London 1911

Barrès, Jean-Baptiste, *Memoirs of a Napoleonic Officer*, London 1925

Belloc, Hilaire, *Napoleon*, London 1932

Blaze, Elzéar, *Military Life Under Napoleon: The Memoirs of Captain Elzéar Blaze*, Chicago 1995 (re-issue, translated by John R. Elting)

Blond, Georges, *La Grande Armée*, London 1997

Bourrienne, F. de, *Memoirs of Napoleon*, London 1905

Chandler, David, *Campaigns of Napoleon*, London 1966

Chandler, David, *Dictionary of the Napoleonic Wars*, London 1979

Chandler, David (ed.), *Napoleon's Marshals*, London 1987

Chlapowski, Dezydery, *Memoirs of a Polish Lancer*, Chicago 1992 (translated by Ted Simmons)

Coignet, Captain Jean-Roch, *Narrative of Captain Coignet: Soldier of the Empire*, London 1897

D'Ideville, Count H. (Charlotte M. Yonge, ed.), *Memoirs of Colonel Bugeaud*, London 1884

Davidov, Denis, *In The Service of the Tsar Against Napoleon: The Memoirs of Denis Davidov 1806–1814*, Translated and Edited by Gregory Troubetzkoy, London 1999

Davies, Norman, *God's Playground,* vol. II, London 2005

Davies, Norman, *Heart of Europe*, London 1984

Davies, Norman, *Microcosm: Portrait of a Central European City*, London 2002

Dunn-Pattison, R.P., *Napoleon's Marshals*, London 1909

Elting, John R., *Swords Around a Throne*, London 1989

Esposito, Vincent J., and Elting, John R., *Military History and Atlas of the Napoleonic Wars*, New York 1964

Fezensac, Raymond Emery Philippe Joseph de Montesquiou, Duc de, *Souvenirs Militaires de 1804 à 1814 par le Duc de Fezensac*, Paris 1870

Foord, Edward, *Napoleon's Russian Campaign of 1812*, London 1914

Foucart, Capitaine P., *Campagne de Pologne*, Paris 1882

Funck, Ferdinand von, *In the Wake of Napoleon*, London 1931

Gallagher, John G., *The Iron Marshal: A Biography of Louis N. Davout*, Edwardsville 1976

Glover, Michael, *Warfare in the Age of Bonaparte*, London 1980

Gonneville, Colonel de (Charlotte M. Yonge, ed.), *Recollections of Colonel de Gonneville*, London 1875

Haffner, Sebastian, *Rise and Fall of Prussia*, London 1980

Haythornthwaite, Philip and Hook, Richard, *Imperial Guardsman 1799–1815*, London 1997

Haythornthwaite, Philip J., *Die Hard: Dramatic Actions From the Napoleonic Wars*, London 1996

Haythornthwaite, Philip J., *Weapons & Equipment of the Napoleonic Wars*, London 1979

Haythornthwaite, Philip J., *Who Was Who in the Napoleonic Wars*, London 1998

Napoleon's Polish Gamble

Henderson, E.F., *Blücher and the Uprising of Prussia Against Napoleon*, London 1911

Herold, Christopher J., *Mind of Napoleon*, New York 1955

Höpfner, E. Von, *Der Krieg von 1806 und 1807*, Berlin 1855

Johnson, David, *French Cavalry 1792–1815*, London 1989

Johnson, David, *Napoleon's Cavalry and its Leaders*, New York 1978

Kukiel, Dr Maryan, *Dzieje Oreza Polskiego w Epoce Napoleonskiej*, Poznan 1912

Lachouque, Henry, and Brown, Anne S.K., *Anatomy of Glory: Napoleon and His Guard*, London 1997

Lejeune, Baron Louis (Mrs A. Bell, ed.), *Memoirs of Baron Lejeune*, London 1897

Leroy-Dupré, L.A.H., *Memoirs of Baron Larrey*, London 1862

Logan, Major F.D., 'Napoleon's Campaign in Poland,' taken from the *Royal Artillery Journal*, 1912–13

MacDonnell, A.G., *Napoleon and His Marshals*, London 1934

McLynn, Frank, *Napoleon: a Biography*, London 1997

Marbot, Baron de (Arthur John Butler, ed.), *Memoirs of Baron de Marbot*, London 1900

Marshall-Cornwall, James, *Napoleon As Military Commander*, London 1967

Nafziger, George F., *Eylau–Friedland Campaign of 1807–07*, West Chester 2003

Norvins, J. de, *Souvenirs d'un Historian de Napoléon*, Paris 1897

Nosworthy, Brent, *Battle Tactics of Napoleon and His Enemies*, London 1995

Palmer, Alan, *Alexander I: Tsar of War and Peace*, London 1974

Palmer, Alan, *Encyclopaedia of Napoleon's Europe*, London 1984

Parker, Harold T., *Three Napoleonic Battles*, Durham 1944

Paulin, General Baron, *Les Souvenirs du Général Baron Paulin*, Paris 1895

Pasquier, *Histoire de Mon Temps*, Paris 1893

Percy, Pierre François, *Journal des Campagnes du Baron Percy, Chirugien en Chef de la Grand Armée, 1757–1825*, Paris 1904

Petre, Loraine F., *Napoleon's Campaign in Poland 1806–07*, London 1901

Rapp, General J., *Memoirs of General Count Rapp, First Aide-de-Camp to Napoleon*, London 1823

Rogacki, Tomasz, *Pruska Ilawa*, Warsaw 2004

Saint-Chamans, General, *Mémoires du Général Comte de Saint-Chamans, Ancien Aide de Camp du Maréchal Soult*, Paris 1896

Savant, Jean, *Napoleon in His Time*, London 1954

Savary, Anne Jean Marie Rene, *Mémoires du Duc de Rovigo*, Paris 1828

Ségur, General Count de, *Aide-de-Camp of Napoleon*, London 1895

Smith, Digby, *Charge: Great Cavalry Charges of the Napoleonic Wars*, London 2003

Smith, Digby, *Napoleonic Wars Data Book*, London 1998

Sutherland, Christine, *Marie Walewska: Napoleon's Great Love*, London 1979

Tascher, Maurice de, *Journal de Campagne d'un Cousin de L'Imperatrice 1806–1813*, Paris 1933

Watson, S.J., *By Command of the Emperor: A Life of Marshal Berthier*, London 1957

Wilson, Sir Robert, *Brief Remarks on the Character and Composition of the Russian Army, and a Sketch of the Campaigns in Poland in the Years 1806 and 1807*, London 1810

Yermolov, Alexei, *The Czar's General: The Memoirs of a Russian General in the Napoleonic Wars*, (translated by Alexander Mikaberidze) Ravenhall Books 2005

Index

Please note: 'Bennigsen', 'Napoleon', 'Poland', 'Prussia', 'Russia', occur too frequently to be included in this index.

167

Napoleon's Polish Gamble